I know not how I shall offend in
slight lines to your Lordship, nor
ill censure mee for choosing so
support so vveake a burthen,
our seeme but pleased, I ac-
d vowe to take aduantage of all
vvith some grauer labour. But
roue deformed, I shall be sorie it
uer after eare so barren a land,
ruest, I leaue it to your Honou-
r hearts contem vvhich I wish
e vvish, and the vvorlds hope-

Your Honors in all dutie,

William Shakespeare.

Henry IV Part two · Act IV. Scene 5.
Prince Henry: "Lo, here it sits,—"

QUOTATIONS FROM
SHAKESPEARE

WITH AN INTRODUCTION AND PREFATORY NOTES BY
PETER QUENNELL

MICHAEL JOSEPH, LONDON

Idea, design and world copyright © 1971
by Tre Tryckare, Gothenburg, Sweden.
B39EN7711

Introduction:
PETER QUENNELL

The illustrations in the
introduction by courtesy of
THE BRITISH BROADCASTING CORPORATION

Drawings by:
ÅKE GUSTAVSSON

The quotations have been selected by
GERTRUD SIMONSSON

In collaboration with
PETER QUENNELL

First published in Great Britain by
MICHAEL JOSEPH LTD
52 Bedford Square
London WC1
1971
Printed in Sweden
SBN 7181 0637 7

INTRODUCTION *by Peter Quennell*

Just over four hundred years ago, on April 22nd or 23rd, 1564, Mary, wife of John Shakespeare, gave birth to their first son; and shortly afterwards they took him to the parish church, where he received the Christian name of William. Stratford-upon-Avon was the Shakespeares' home, Warwickshire their native county. John ranked as an important citizen of Stratford; and, when William was four years old, he became its mayor or "bailiff". True, he presently began to lose money, was deprived of the respectable status of alderman and, because he feared that he might be arrested for debt, could seldom leave his own house; but his Stratfordian neighbours seem to have liked him; and, in his later years, he is said to have been a "merry-cheeked old man", who once remarked that his famous son Will was a "good honest fellow", with whom he never feared to crack a joke.

Such were the origins of our greatest English poet and playwright. And here I must express my firm conviction that the poems and plays attributed to William Shakespeare were indeed the original work of John Shakespeare's son; that there is no demonstrable reason why he should not have written them; finally, that every attempt to make out a case for another poet — or group of poets — involves far more serious difficulties, both critical and historical, than does a straightforward acceptance of the Stratfordian playwright's claim.

Facsimile of entry in the baptismal register in Stratford.

It is disappointing, of course, that we should know so little about Shakespeare — about some contemporary dramatists we know even less; but the information that *has* come down to us is far more extensive than many modern critics have suggested. It has been said that everything we know of his life and character could be written on a postcard. Well, to that I can only reply that it would have to be a very large postcard, and that the writer would have to employ an almost microscopic script. We learn a great deal about his public doings, his professional career, the properties in which he invested his earnings as a successful dramatist and actor-manager, and where he lived at different stages of his life. We have also numerous references, by those who knew him well, to his private character and growing literary reputation. During his lifetime, no one suspected — or so much as hinted at

Family worship in the Tudor period. Book illustration from 1563.

a suspicion — that William Shakespeare of London and Stratford was not the real author of the dramatic masterpieces eventually collected in the First Folio.

Admittedly, his youth remains obscure. We cannot tell exactly where he was educated; and all we can say is that the son of a member of the Stratford Council would almost certainly have been enrolled at the local Grammar School, and would have there received tuition free; and Stratford Grammar School, like other Elizabethan establishments of the same kind, offered its pupils a sound modern training — in Latin if not in Greek, and in grammar, logic and the fashionable art of rhetoric, with arithmatic, geometry, astronomy and music thrown in to supply the necessary balance.

The author of the plays was no deep classical scholar — he left that to his rival Ben Jonson; but clearly he was a well-educated man; and at some period of his existence he had evidently made a study of the law. Hence the story that, after he had grown up, he earned his living in a lawyer's office. At the same time, it is thought that he may have been a country schoolmaster. These theories depend on guesswork. We know, however, that, towards the end of the year 1582, while he was still living at Stratford, he contracted — or perhaps was forced into — a somewhat undignified and hurried marriage. His wife, Anne Hathaway, was eight years older than himself and, when she became his wife, already pregnant. She gave birth to her first child, Susanna, in May, 1583.

There follows a considerable gap in the record. Twin children, Hamnet and Judith, were born to William and Anne Shakespeare in January, 1585; and, for what it is worth, we have the well-known tale that Shakespeare was obliged to leave Stratford and his family, and "shelter himself in London", as the result of some "extravagances" connected with the theft of game. He is reputed to have broken into a neighbouring park, and there run wild among the deer or rabbits.

Our real knowledge of Shakespeare begins as late as 1592. By now the young Stratfordian had gained a foothold in London, and was apprenticed to the stage both as a player and a dramatist. He had been put to work on a popular historical play, chronicling the disastrous reign of King Henry VI; and his efforts had had sufficient success to enrage an unhappy fellow poet. Robert Greene was ill and ageing and embittered; and, when he died, he left behind him a pamphlet, in which, besides attacking the vices of the stage and warning his associates against its pitfalls, he singled out a certain ambitious and unscrupulous young man who had thrust himself into public view by plagiarising

The Globe Theatre in London. Around 1616.

Interior view of the old Swan Theatre. Drawing by the Dutchman Jan de Witt, 1596.

Caricature by Robert Greene. Frontispiece of a pamphlet of 1593.

other men's verses — "an upstart crow, beautified with our feathers that . . . supposes he is as well able to bombast out a blank verse as the best of you, and, being an absolute *Johannes fac totum,* is in his own conceit the only Shake-scene in a country . . ."

The attack was significant. Still more significant was the response that it elicited. Henry Chettle, who had been responsible for the publication of Greene's posthumous diatribe, produced another pamphlet, *Kindheart's Dream,* in which he did his best to make amends. He was sorry, he announced, to have offended a living poet, "because myself have seen his demeanour no less civil than he excellent in the quality he professes. Besides, divers of worship have reported his uprightness of dealing, which argues his honesty, and his facetious grace that approves his art".

The tributes that Chettle pays to the twenty-eight-year-old Shakespeare — "civil", "upright", "honest" — are repeated in the long series of tributes that he continued to elicit throughout his lifetime. They are échoed, for example, by Ben Jonson. Shakespeare, we learn, was "friendly", "gentle", "sweet". He had

9

Portrait of Shakespeare in his youth, probably from 1597.

"loved the man", declared Jonson ". . . He was, indeed, honest, and of an open and free nature: had an excellent Fancy, brave notions and gentle expressions . . ." Shakespeare, moreover, would appear to have been a physically attractive person. "He was a handsome, well-shaped man", reports the seventeenth-century gossip-writer John Aubrey, "and of a very ready and pleasant, smooth wit".

Apart from this, when we are trying to form a personal impression of Shakespeare, we have the evidence of his own works. Although a Londoner by adoption, he was still deeply attached to the country and to his recollections of his country childhood. He understood the points of a good horse — as we see from his celebrated description of a "well-proportioned steed" in *Venus and Adonis;* and the same poem, with his description of a hunted hare, shows that Shakespeare must often have risen early to follow the harriers across the fields. He had a deep imaginative feeling for the life of beasts and birds — the mallard in the Warwickshire water-meadows; the "dabchick", or little grebe; even the timid snail amid the grass-stalks.

Shakespeare also delighted in the company of women and children, and loved to talk to them, and hear them talk. Of his marriage we know almost nothing. Perhaps he would have agreed with the great French cynic La Rochefoucauld that "there are tolerable marriages, but no delicious ones"; and twice — in *Henry VI, Part I*, and, much later, in *The Tempest* — he writes of the horrors that attend unwilling wedlock:

> *For what is wedlock forcéd but a hell,*
> *An age of discord and continual strife?*

Nevertheless, he was clearly devoted to women — particularly to young and rather boyish women; and

Hunting with falcons. Old woodcut by Turberville, 1578.

he was exquisitely sensitive to physical beauty — to the charm of dark eyes, a "velvet brow", and a fine transparent skin "laced with blue of heaven's own tinct". But, although his tastes were active and energetic, and he was a man of the world who relished worldly pleasures, he had a contemplative and introspective side. Like Shelley and Byron, he was fascinated by water; and, with his elbows on the parapet of Stratford's ancient Clopton Bridge, must often have gazed down at a swan's feather caught in the eddying current of the Avon; while, as an older man, travelling around England with the theatrical company he had joined, again and again he must have climbed some headland and looked forth on to a stormy sea or, when the ocean was calm, listened to the waves below chafing "th' unnumbered idle pebble".

Shakespeare was plainly a well-organized character — active yet contemplative, industrious yet pleasure-loving. What is more, he was blessed with luck; and perhaps one of his greatest strokes of good fortune was the early death of Christopher Marlowe. Already, in 1587, Marlowe's tremendous *Tamburlaine* had electrified a London audience, and had revealed that mastery of the "mighty line" which transfigured English blank-verse drama. But, in 1593, Marlowe met a violent end; and his death removed from the scene a formidable poetic rival — all the more to be feared since his gifts and character were so very different.

It was during the year of Marlowe's death that Shakespeare gained an influential patron — presumably one of the "persons of worship" mentioned by Henry Chettle in his *Kindheart's Dream*. In 1593 he dedicated his decorative Ovidian poem, *Venus and Adonis*, to a handsome twenty-year-old courtier, Henry Wriothesley, Earl of Southampton; and, a year later, he addressed a second poem, *The Rape of*

Lady with rose. Print for the series "The Five Senses" by Crispin de Passe (1550-1643, approx.).

Lucrece, with a no less complimentary, but somewhat more personal form of dedication, to the same attractive young grandee.

Shakespeare had chosen his patron wisely. Not only was Southampton one of the most brilliant of Queen Elizabeth's many brilliant young men, and reputed to be a "dear lover and cherisher of poets", but he was closely connected with the Earl of Essex, now a powerful royal favourite, and among the strangest and most fascinating figures of the whole Elizabethan Age. The

*Portrait of the
young Henry Wriothesly,
Earl of Southampton.*

story told in the *Sonnets* (which Shakespeare may have begun to write about 1594) has never been finally elucidated. Some critics believe that the young man whom the poet idolised was probably Lord Pembroke. I am myself convinced that this "golden youth" was certainly his early patron; that, through Southampton, he came to know Essex; and that it was the tragedy of Essex's decline and fall that launched the dramatist into the composition of his noblest tragedies, the dramas of the so-called "Dark Period", when he produced in rapid succession *Julius Caesar, Troilus and Cressida, Hamlet, Antony and Cleopatra, Coriolanus.*

So far I have dealt with a single aspect of Shakespeare's richly complex nature. I have examined "friendly Shakespeare", "gentle Shakespeare", the poet who was also a successful careerist, who restored his family's fortunes, procured his father a brand-new coat of arms, made some shrewd financial investments and at length bought the largest house in Stratford. Such was the Shakespeare portrayed by Droeshout, when he executed the well-known portrait that appears as frontispiece to the First Folio.

That portrait has often been criticised, and, though it seems to incorporate a perfectly good likeness, has been dismissed as dull and wooden. One anti-Stratfordian has gone so far as to suggest that what it shows is not a living face but the portrait of a man who wears a mask — a mask that conceals the poet's real identity. This is ridiculous. Yet, in another and wider sense, Shakespeare may indeed have worn a mask. "Friendly Shakespeare" may have been the artist's *persona*; and underneath that amiable, worldly disguise may have lurked a very different set of features.

Potentially, if not actually, he was both a neurotic and a melancholic. Many of the greatest works of imaginative art seem to have owed their origins to some hidden conflict; and the author of Shakespeare's tragedies was neither a simple nor a self-complacent man. Here, as elsewhere, we can only rely on guess-work; but his childhood must undoubtedly have been overshadowed by his father's long financial struggles, and by the feelings of mingled loyalty and resentment they aroused in his ambitious son. Incidentally, there was a galling social contrast between his father's and his mother's origins. John Shakespeare came of sober middle-class stock. Mary was descended from the comparatively prosperous and well-born Ardens.

However the basic conflict arose, Shakespeare had a sharply divided nature. He was cheerful, good-humoured, gregarious; but through his tragedies — and, indeed, through some of his comedies — runs the poignant theme of individual isolation. It begins to appear as early as Richard III, the picture of a tyrant

Terpsichore, the Muse of Dancing. Print from the series "The Muses" by Crispin de Passe (1550-1643, approx.).

tormented now by furious self-love, now by passionate hatred:

> *Richard loves Richard; that is, I am I.*
> *Is there a murderer here? No — yes, I am:*
> *Then fly. What, from myself? Great reason why —*
> *Lest I revenge. Myself upon myself?*
> *Alack, I love myself. For any good*
> *That I myself have done unto myself?*

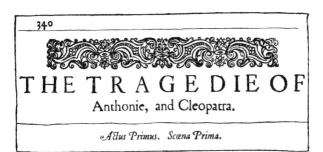

THE TRAGEDIE OF
Anthonie, and Cleopatra.

Actus Primus. Scœna Prima.

Facsimile of main title of "Antony and Cleopatra" from the 1623 folio edition.

All his subsequent tragic heroes — and I regard Shylock as a tragic figure, and Malvolio as a tragic personage displayed from a comic point of view — are lonely, self-secluded men, cut off by some passion or obsession that makes it impossible for them to communicate freely with their fellow human beings. Thus Hamlet is the victim of his sense of intellectual strength and moral weakness: Othello and Antony, of their rebellious lusts. Macbeth is brought down by the slow accumulation of guilt: Coriolanus, by his over-weening pride. Each of them stands alone; each, as the tragedy develops, finds that his solipsistic solitude has at length become a prison; each is destined to die alone, without any religious hope of reconciliation or atonement.

Shakespeare, no doubt, was a practising Christian. But can we feel sure that he embraced the Christian *ethos?* Did he accept the doctrine of personal immortality? Hamlet's friend invokes a flight of angels to follow his "sweet prince" through the gates of death; but Hamlet himself declares that "the rest is silence";

and a similar hush descends upon the conclusion of the other tragedies. The dramatist, we know, was a student of Montaigne, whose English translator, John Florio, was a member of the Essex-Southampton circle; and, if he can be said to have a moral philosophy, it is the pagan stoicism that Montaigne teaches. Man must be true to himself; *"Man must endure . . ."* That precept, delivered with supreme eloquence in one of the latter scenes of *King Lear,* is almost his only philosophic message.

Shakespeare's own attitude towards human life, so far as we can divine it from his works, was curiously ambivalent. He loved life; and he feared and hated life. No poet has written more feelingly of the physical

Pair of lovers. Print from "The Ages of Man" by Crispin de Passe (1550-1643 approx.).

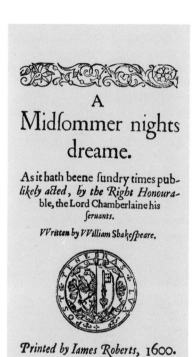

A
Midſommer nights
dreame.

As it hath beene ſundry times pub-
likely acted, by the Right Honoura-
ble, the Lord Chamberlaine his
ſeruants.

VVritten by VVilliam Shakeſpeare.

Printed by Iames Roberts, 1600.

*Facsimile of the
title page of
"A Midsummer
Night's Dream",
1600. In the 1619
reprint. Date
misprinted.*

beauties of the sensuous world — of the charm of
human flesh and blood, of the splendid procession of
the seasons, of the loveliness of fields and flowers. He
had the Renaissance respect for Man as the apex of
creation, a deep regard for human dignity. Yet Man
is also a "poor forked animal", chance product of
"our dungy earth".

And then, while Shakespeare — the Shakespeare of
Stratford-upon-Avon and the London playhouses —
had both feet firmly planted on the ground, Shakespeare the poet would seem often to have doubted the

solid actuality of the material universe. He was obsessed by the idea of life-as-a-dream; and not only did he write *A Midsummer Night's Dream* — in which the various modes of loving are represented as varying types of folly and illusion — but he created Macbeth, for whom human life is an ill-acted play, and Antony, who, at the moment of death, feels that he is losing all sense of his own physical reality:

Sometime we see a cloud that's dragonish,
A vapour sometime like a bear or lion,
A towered citadel, a pendant rock,
A forked mountain, or blue promontory . . .
That which is now a horse, even with a thought,
The rack dislimns, and makes it indistinct
As water is in water . . .
My good knave Eros, now thy captain is
Even such a body: here I am Antony
Yet cannot hold this visible shape, my knave.

A reader may object here that it is equally dangerous and wrong to identify the words that a dramatist gives his dramatic personae with the opinions that he holds himself. But surely no one could have written the great tragedies whose own view of life was not profoundly tragic; and Shakespeare's mood, before he retired into private existence, may be attributed to several different causes. His only son, Hamnet, died at the age of eleven, in August 1596; and *King John,* the play he was then writing, contains a poignant reference to a child's extinction. *King John* also introduces the theme that he was to enlarge upon in later tragedies. Human life is not only cruel and meaningless, but wearisome and insignificant:

Life is as tedious as a twice-told tale
Vexing the dull ear of a drowsy man.

121

T'IS better to be vile then vile esteemed,
When not to be,receiues reproach of being,
And the iust pleasure lost,which is so deemed,
Not by our feeling,but by others seeing.
For why should others false adulterat eyes
Giue salutation to my sportiue blood?
Or on my frailties why are frailer spies;
Which in their wils count bad what I think good?
Noe, I am that I am,and they that leuell
At my abuses,reckon vp their owne,
I may be straight though they them-selues be beuel
By their rancke thoughtes,my deedes must not be showne
    Vnlesse this generall euill they maintaine,
    All men are bad and in their badnesse raigne.

Facsimile of Sonnet 121.

The second crisis in Shakespeare's private life was connected, we may assume with the secret history of the *Sonnets*. This is not the place to enter into the controversy that these mysterious poems have long aroused, and still arouse, nor to discuss the printer's enigmatic dedication to an unidentified "Mr. W.H." There is no doubt, however, that they are intensely personal poems and depict some disastrous upheaval in the poet's private life; that he was deeply devoted to a handsome, capricious, extravagant young man — "the man right fair", just such a youth as Lord Southampton; and that simultaneously he had a dark deceitful mistress, who betrayed him with the friend he idolised. The youth represented romantic platonic love; the "Dark Lady" stood for sensual passion, against which he was perpetually revolting, but from which he could never quite escape.

Queen Elizabeth I.

That episode may well have overshadowed the middle period of Shakespeare's life, from 1593, when he first encountered Southampton until the beginning of the next century. If he loved Southampton, he must have admired Essex, a character who bore some resemblance to Hamlet — learned, charming, accomplished, yet, like the Prince of Denmark, neurasthenic and irresolute; a man with lofty aims and high ideals, which he failed to translate into concrete action. During the last years of Queen Elizabeth's reign, many shadows were gathering in the sky. At home, there was widespread unemployment; abroad, in Ireland

and France, England fought costly and inconclusive wars. The Queen and the House of Commons were often at variance; and the problem of the succession — Elizabeth, though now an old women, obstinately refused to name her heir — kept the politicians' nerves on edge.

Against this gloomy background Essex stood forth as a gallant, gifted and disinterested leader, a spokesman of the young and a chivalrous champion of the common people, the only public figure, except for the Queen, to whom Shakespeare makes a flattering reference. Essex, he prophesied in *Henry V,* would return a conquering hero from the Irish Wars. But Essex's attempt to subdue the rebels proved an ignominious failure. He was disgraced and imprisoned, and, soon after his release, launched an armed revolt against the Queen's entourage. Again he failed, and he was promptly sentenced to death; while Southampton, his fellow conspirator, was condemned to life-imprisonment — but not before Essex had made an abject act of repentance, and Southampton had pleaded "submissively" for his life and callously renounced his former friend.

Their joint fall — or so I believe — left the poet a prematurely embittered and disillusioned man. The lion had fallen: the fox, prevailed. Everywhere he looked, he saw cowardice, selfishness, vulgar egotism and material greed. Shakespeare had always appreciated valiant, handsome men of action. Now the more he saw of them, the less he trusted them. They were "dragonish clouds", shadowy, insubstantial wraiths, which he had once been foolish enough to mistake for the solid forms of kings and heroes. During the Dark Period, every man of action he describes is eventually betrayed or at length betrays himself. This was the period of *Troilus and Cressida,* in which Achilles — to whom Essex had once been likened — is written off as the "idol of idiot-worshippers", an arrogant, evil-tempered booby.

So far I have dwelt on the more negative aspects of Shakespeare's character — on his pessimism, his anxieties and fears — rather than on his immense creative genius. I have said nothing of the exquisite beauty of his songs, the lyrical spirit of his comedies, the dignity and strength of his great historic dramas. The point I wish to make is that, if Shakespeare can be acclaimed as a poet of universal gifts, it was because he maintained so nice a balance between two opposing states of mind. He understood the zest and the joy of life as well as he understood the horror and the pain of living. In other dramas — those of Strindberg, for example — we find pessimism almost unrelieved. A Shakespearian tragedy includes so many elements — so much of human life, so strongly combined and worked together into so rich a whole — that, even at its most terrible, the effect produced is somehow majestic and inspiriting. We never quite lose our faith in Man. Shakespeare was a Renaissance humanist, for whom Man, however deluded and misguided, was still creation's finest work.

His humanism is implicit both in his tragedies and in his comedies; and very often the personages he exalts are those who, when he began to write, he may have intended to abuse or ridicule. His plays are full of "runaway characters" who break through the framework of his original design — Shylock who enters the play, as a villainous miscreant, but soon assumes an air of tragic dignity; Falstaff, a comic bufoon, who gradually pushes aside his fellow characters and strides into the centre of the stage. Unlike Christopher Marlowe, Shakespeare was not a revolutionary poet. So far as we can tell, he was by temperament a staunch conservative, and accepted the

Elizabethan doctrine of "degree" that allotted every human being, and every animal or plant, a predestined place in the eternal scheme. Nor was Shakespeare concerned with the important scientific discoveries that we owe to sixteenth-century men of learning. He paid no attention to the new Copernican theories that had displaced the terrestial universe, and ridiculed the modern scientist's attempts to name the stars and chart their courses:

> *Those earthly godfathers of heaven's lights,*
> *That give a name to every fixéd star,*
> *Have no more profit of their shining nights*
> *Than those that walk and wot not what they are.*

On one plane, William Shakespeare was a shrewd commercial dramatist, who wrote to satisfy contemporary demands, producing two elaborate Ovidian poems when that type of verse was particularly fashionable; turning out a series of impressive historical plays when the defeat of the Armada had inspired the Elizabethans with a passionate interest in their own history; and writing a series of romantic comedies, presenting gay, well-born young men and delightful boyish girls, calculated to please Southampton, Essex and their frivolous patrician households.

It is among the miracles of Shakespeare's achievement that, although he apparently submitted and conformed, he rose so high above his audience; and that he was able to do what his *genius* dictated, while, for the benefit of the contemporary public, he employed his *talents,* which were themselves astonishing, to the utmost practical advantage. Shakespeare undoubtedly was a man of his age. Yet, having transcended that age's limitations, he became an "everliving" artist.

The Tempest · Act I. Scene 2.

*Prospero: "Thou most lying slave, whom stripes may move,
not kindness . . ."*

THE TEMPEST

Described by William Hazlitt as "one of the most original and perfect" of Shakespeare's productions — a play in which he showed his full "variety of powers" — *The Tempest* was acted before King James I at Whitehall by the playwright's own theatrical company, the King's Players, on November 1st, 1611. The dramatic taste of the age was changing; and, to satisfy that taste, Shakespeare includes a series of masques and shows, with songs that a court-composer set to music. Victorian writers would have had us believe that it was the poet's farewell: like Prospero, he was bidding the world goodbye, drowning his books and casting off his magic robes. But Prospero's mood is far from benevolent; "there is no character in the play", observed Lytton Strachey, "to whom, during some part of it, he is not studiously disagreeable". He bullies and threatens the young prince; Ariel respects but fears him; he terrorises his servant Caliban, "a savage and deformed slave". Again, Shakespeare returns to the idea of life-as-a-dream; and Prospero, in his magnificent valedictory speech —

"Our revels now are ended . . ."

suggests that human life and the whole surrounding universe may be no more than an "insubstantial pageant", which will presently dissolve and leave behind no trace. From a poetic point of view, *The Tempest* is Shakespeare's finest comedy, in which tragic undertones are relieved by passages of exquisite lyrical charm. The songs are justly celebrated. Prospero's island is indeed a place of enchantment; and Miranda, awakening to a "brave new world" and, as she gazes for the first time at a young man's face, exclaiming delightedly: "How beauteous mankind is!", has the freshness and charm of Shakespeare's earlier heroines, without any of their aggressive pertness. Evidently the poet continued to love the world. His last comedy sums up an attitude towards life in which loving and loathing hold an even balance.

THE TEMPEST

Act I · Scene 1

Boatswain: Heigh, my hearts! cheerly, cheerly, my hearts! yare, yare! Take in the topsail! 'Tend to the master's whistle! — Blow, till thou burst thy wind, if room enough!

Gonzalo: Good, yet remember whom you hast aboard.
Boatswain: None that I more love than myself.

Gonzalo: Now would I give a thousand furlongs of sea for an acre of barren ground;

Gonzalo: But I would fain die a dry death.

THE TEMPEST

Act I · Scene 2

Prospero: *He being thus lorded,*
Not only with what my revenue yielded,
But what my power might else exact, — like one,
Who having, unto truth, by telling of it,
Made such a sinner of his memory,
To credit his own lie,

Prospero: Me, poor man! — my library
Was dukedom large enough;

Miranda: O, I have suffer'd
With those that I saw suffer!
A brave vessel,
Who had, no doubt, some noble creature in her,
Dash'd all to pieces. O, the cry did knock
Against my very heart! Poor souls, the perish'd.

THE TEMPEST

Act I · Scene 2

Prospero: *No harm*
I have done nothing but in care of thee;
(Of thee, my dear one, thee, my daughter) who
Art ignorant of what thou art, naught knowing
Of whence I am; nor that I am more better
Than Prospero, master of a full poor cell,
And thy no greater father.

Miranda: I should sin
To think but nobly of my grandmother:
Good wombs have borne bad sons.

Prospero: A rotten carcass of a boat,

— — —

The very rats
Instinctively had quit it:

Ariel (sings): Full fathom five thy father lies;
Of his bones are coral made;
Those are pearls that were his eyes:
Nothing of him that doth fade,
But doth suffer a sea-change
Into something rich and strange.

Prospero: This swift business
I must uneasy make, lest too light winning
Make the prize light.

THE TEMPEST

Act II · Scene 1

Prospero: Thou art inclin'd to sleep; 'tis a good dulness,
And give it way; I know thou canst not choose.

Sebastian: Look, he's winding up the watch of his wit;
By and by it will strike.

THE TEMPEST

Act II · Scene 1

Gonzalo: When every grief is entertain'd that's offer'd.
Comes to the entertainer —
Sebastian: A dollar
Gonzalo: Dolour comes to him, indeed; you have
spoken truer than you purposed.

Sebastian: He receives comfort like cold porridge.

Sebastian: Hereditary sloth instructs me.

— — —

Antonio: Ebbing men, indeed,
Most often do so near the bottom run,
By their own fear, or sloth.

Gonzalo: Here is everything advantageous to life.
Antonio: True; save means to live

THE TEMPEST

Act II · Scene I

Antonio: O, out of that "no hope"
What great hope have you! no hope, that way, is
Another way so high an hope that even
Ambition cannot pierce a wink beyond,
But doubts discovery there. Will you grant with me
That Ferdinand is drown'd?
Sebastian: He's gone.

Sebastian: But, for your conscience —
Antonio: Ay, sir; where lies that? if it were a kybe,
'Twould put me to my slipper: But I feel not
This deity in my bosom; twenty consciences,
That stand 'twixt me and Milan, candied be they,
And melt, ere they molest! Here lies your brother,
No better than the earth he lies upon,
If he were that which now he's like: whom I,
With this obedient steel, three inches of it,
Can lay to bed for ever: whiles you, doing thus
To the perpetual wink for aye might put
This ancient morsel, this Sir Prudence, who
Should not upbraid our course. For all the rest,
They'll take suggestions, as a cat laps milk;
They'll tell the clock to any business that
We say befits the hour.

THE TEMPEST

Act II · Scene 2

Trinculo: Misery acquaints a man
with strange bedfellows.

Caliban: I pr'ythee, let me bring thee where crabs
grow;
And I with my long nails will dig thee pig-nuts;
Show thee a jay's nest, and instruct thee how
To snare the nimble marmozet; I'll bring thee
To clustering filberts, and sometimes I'll get thee
Young sea-mells from the rock,
Wilt thou go with me?

THE TEMPEST

Act III · Scene 1

Ferdinand: *Admir'd Miranda!*
Indeed the top of admiration;
What's dearest to the world! Full many a lady
I have eyed with best regard; and many a time
The harmony of their tongues hath into bondage
Brought my too diligent ear; for several virtues
Have I lik'd several women; never any
With so full soul, but some defect in her
Did quarrel with the noblest grace she owed,
And put it to the foil; but you,
O you,
So perfect and so peerless, are created
Of every creature's best.

THE TEMPEST

Act III · Scene 2

Caliban: Be not afeard; the isle is full of noises,
Sounds, and sweet airs, that give delight and hurt not.
Sometimes a thousand twangling instruments
Will hum about mine ears; and sometimes voices,
That, if I then had waked after long sleep,
Will make me sleep again; and then, in dreaming,
The clouds, methought, would open and show riches
Ready to drop upon me: that, when I waked,
I cried to dream again.

Act III · Scene 3

Ariel: You fools! I and my fellows
Are ministers of fate: the elements,
Of whom your swords are temper'd, may as well
Wound the loud winds, or with bemock'd-at stabs
Kill the still-closing waters, as diminish
One dowle that's in my plume;
My fellow ministers
Are like invulnerable.

THE TEMPEST

Act IV · Scene I

Ariel: Before you can say, "Come and Go",
And breathe twice; and cry "So, so";
Each one, tripping on his toe,
Will be here with mop and mow:
Do you love me, master? no?

Caliban: And all be turned to barnacles, or to apes
With foreheads villanous low.

Prospero: Our revels are now ended: these our actors,
As I foretold you, were all spirits, and
Are melted into air, into thin air:
And, like the baseless fabric of this vision
The cloud-capp'd towers, the gorgeous palaces,
The solemn temples, the great globe itself,
Yea, all which it inherit, shall dissolve,
And, like this insubstantial pageant faded.
Leave not a rack behind: We are such stuff
As dreams are made on, and our little life
Is rounded with a sleep.

THE TEMPEST

Act V · Scene 1

Prospero: Ye elves of hills, brooks, standing lakes,
*   and groves;*
And ye that on the sands with printless foot
Do chase the ebbing Neptune, and do fly him
When he comes back; you demi-puppets that
By moonshine do the green sour ringlets make,
Whereof the ewe not bites;
— — —

Weak masters though ye be, — I have bedimm'd
The noontide sun, call'd for the mutinous winds,

Ariel (sings): Where the bee sucks, there suck I;
*   In a cowslip's bell I lie;*
*   There I couch when owls do cry.*
*   On the bat's back I do fly*
*   After summer merrily:*

Prospero: Though with their high wrongs I am struck
*   to the quick,*
Yet, with my noble reason, 'gainst my fury
Do I take part: the rarer action is
In virtue than in vengeance:

Alonso: How thou hast met us here, who three hours
*   since*
Were wreck'd upon this shore; where I have lost —
How sharp the point of this remembrance is! —
Me dear son Ferdinand.

THE TEMPEST

Act V · Scene 1

Prospero: Let us not burden our remembrances
With a heaviness that's gone.

Trinculo: I have been in such a pickle since I saw you
      last

Miranda: O, wonder!
How many goodly creatures are there here!
How beauteous mankind is! O brave new world,
That hath such people in't!

Prospero: A solemn air, and the best comforter
To an unsettled fancy, cure thy brains,

Epilogue spoken by Prospero:

Now my charms are all o'erthrown,
And what strength I have's mine own, —
Which is most faint: now 'tis true,
I must be here confined by you,
Or sent to Naples. Let me not,
Since I have my dukedom got,
And pardon'd the deceiver, dwell
In this bare island by your spell;
— — —

As you from crimes would pardon'd be,
Let your indulgence set me free.

THE TWO GENTLEMEN OF VERONA

Shakespeare was no isolated intellectual, but a hard-pressed working dramatist; and he had not only to suit his audience's tastes but to make the fullest use that he could of the talents of his fellow actors. Some of those actors were boys, carefully schooled to act in women's parts; and their popularity had a very marked effect upon the writing of his romantic comedies. In such plays his heroines are apt to reveal a curiously bisexual character — feminine yet at the same time boyish, now modest and retiring, now bold, talkative and self-assertive. One of the first of these transvestite heroines was Julia in *The Two Gentlemen of Verona*. Probably written before 1594, it has been described as "having claims to be considered Shakespeare's most tedious play". Certainly the plot is awkward and far-fetched. But, although it ranks among the poet's prentice works, it includes passages of great lyric beauty. Thus Julia compares her passion to a stream carrying her along towards her lover:

> *The current that with gentle murmur glides,*
> *Thou know'st, being stopped, impatiently doth rage:*
> *But when his fair is not hindered,*
> *He makes sweet music with th'enamelled stones . . .*
> *Then let me go, and hinder not my course:*
> *I'll be as patient as a gentle stream,*
> *And make a pastime of each weary step,*
> *Till the last step have brought me to my love.*

Another boy-comedian took the part of her maid Lucetta; and Lucetta had the bawdy turn of wit that, in the Elizabethan playhouse, never failed to raise a laugh.

THE TWO GENTLEMEN OF VERONA

Act I · Scene 1

Valentine: Home-keeping youth hath ever homely wits;
Wer't not affection chains they tender days
To the sweet glances of they honour'd love,
I rather would entreat thy company
To see the wonders of the world abroad,

Proteus: He after honour hunts, I after love;
He leaves his friends to dignify them more;
I leave myself, my friends, and all, for love.
Thou, Julia, thou has metamorphos'd me;
Made me neglect my studies, lose my time,
War with good counsel, set the world at naught.

Two Gentlemen of Verona · Act II. Scene 7.

Lucetta: "What fashion, madam, shall I make your breeches?"

THE TWO GENTLEMEN OF VERONA

Act I · Scene 3

Antonio: I have consider'd well his loss of time,
And how he cannot be a perfect man,
Not being tried and tutor'd in the world:
Experience is by industry achieved.
And perfected by the swift course of time.

Proteus: O, how this spring of love resembleth
The uncertain glory of an April day;
Which now shows all the beauty of the sun,
And by and by a cloud takes all away!

Act II · Scene 2

Proteus: What, gone without a word?
Ay; so true love should do; it cannot speak;
For truth hath better deeds than words to grace it.

THE TWO GENTLEMEN OF VERONA

Act II · Scene 3

*Launce: I think Crab my dog be the sourest-natured
dog that lives: my mother weeping, my father wailing,
my sister crying, our maid howling, our cat wringing
her hands, and all our house in a great perplexity; yet
did not this cruel-hearted cur shed one tear: he is a
stone, a very pebble-stone, and has no more pity in
him than a dog.*

*Lucetta: I do not seek to quench your love's hot fire;
But qualify the fire's extreme rage,
Lest it should burn above the bounds of reason.*

*Julia: The more thou damm'st it up, the more it burns;
The current that with gentle murmur glides,
Thou know'st, being stopp'd, impatiently doth rage;
But when his fair course is not hindered,
He makes sweet music with the enammell'd stones,
Giving a gentle kiss to every sedge
He overtaketh in his pilgrimage;
And so by many winding nooks he strays,
With willing sport, to the wild ocean.
Then let me go, and hinder not my course:
I'll be as patient as a gentle stream,
And make a pastime of each weary step,
Till the last step have brought me to my love;*

THE TWO GENTLEMEN OF VERONA

Act III · Scene 1

Proteus: Cease to lament for that thou canst not help,
And study help for that which thou lament'st.
Time is the nurse and breeder of all good.
— — —
Hope is a lover's staff; walk hence with that,
And manage it against despairing thoughts.

Act III · Scene 2

Proteus: The best way is to slander Valentine
With falsehood, cowardice, and poor descent;
Three things that women highly hold in hate.

Act V · Scene 4

Valentine: How use doth breed a habit in a man!
This shadowy desert, unfrequented woods,
I better brook than flourishing peopled towns:
Here can I sit alone, unseen of any,
And to the nightingale's complaining notes
Tune my distresses and record my woes.

The Merry Wives of Windsor · Act III. Scene 3.

Falstaff: "What made me love thee?"

THE MERRY WIVES OF WINDSOR

According to an attractive, though unauthenticated story, Shakespeare wrote *The Merry Wives of Windsor* about 1600 or 1601 at the request of Queen Elizabeth herself, who desired him to produce a play showing Sir John Falstaff in the rôle of lover. Falstaff by this time was an established comic personage, who had grown as real to the Elizabethans as some of Charles Dickens' creations would become to his Victorian readers. But Shakespeare revived him on a less heroic scale; Falstaff in Henry IV is always the master of the situation, soldier, courtier and experienced amorist, respected by his pot-house cronies, loved by Doll Tearsheet and adored by Mistress Quickly. In *The Merry Wives* he appears as a figure of fun. He has not, however, lost his eloquence: and his account of how he was imprisoned in a basket of dirty linen, and plunged "hissing hot" into the Thames, is a minor masterpiece of comic narrative. The play, incidentally, contains some references to Shakespeare's youth at Stratford. The coat-of-arms of Sir Thomas Lucy, the local landowner and Justice of the Peace, whose game the young man is said to have poached, provide Sir Hugh Evans with a characteristic pun; while Sir Hugh, the garrulous Welshman, is believed to have been drawn from his memories of Thomas Jenkins, a Welsh pedagogue who joined Stratford Grammar School in 1577, when Shakespeare was thirteen years old.

THE MERRY WIVES OF WINDSOR

Act I · Scene 1

Slender: But if there be no great love in the beginning, yet Heaven may decrease it upon better acquaintance, when we are married, and have more occasion to know one another.

Act II · Scene 2

Falstaff: Of what quality was your love, then?
Ford: Like a fair house built on another man's ground; so that I have lost my edifice by mistaking the place where I erected it.

THE MERRY WIVES OF WINDSOR

Act III · Scene 3

Falstaff: What made me love thee? Let that persuade thee, there's something extraordinary in thee. Come, I cannot cog, and say thou art this and that, like a many of these lisping hawthorn buds that come like women in men's apparel, and smell like Buckler's-bury in simple time.

Act V̄ · Scene 5

Falstaff: Remember, Jove, thou wast a bull for thy Europa; love set on thy horns — O powerful love! that, in some respects, makes a beast a man; in some other, a man a beast. You were also Jupiter, a swan, for the love of Leda: O omnipotent love! how near the god drew to the complexion of a goose?

Measure for Measure · Act III. Scene 1.

Isabella: "Yes, brother, you may live . . ."

MEASURE FOR MEASURE

There is one school of Shakespearian critics who find it nearly impossible to admit that the great man ever nodded; any flaw that appears in his workmanship must, they feel, have been intentional. From the commonsense point of view *Measure for Measure* is an ill-constructed play. Shakespeare begins by building up an intensely dramatic situation; Isabella is required to choose between her own dishonour and her brother Claudio's death; and Claudio at first agrees to die, then rejects her pleadings and begs her to let him live. Their persecutor, the corrupt moralist who has pronounced Claudio's doom, is himself a fascinating psychological study. Here Shakespeare's interest in his personages seems suddenly to fall off; art is replaced by artifice; and villainy is punished and virtue rewarded with the help of many curious stratagems. Out of these last episodes some critics have attempted to extract a deep moral and relgious message. Such exegesis fails to take into account the conditions in which Shakespeare lived and laboured. May not his writing of the play have been interrupted; with the result that, when he took it up again, he discovered that he could no longer continue his work upon the same dramatic level? Whatever the explanation, *Measure for Measure* produces a somewhat fragmentary effect; and only the incomparable opening scenes bear the authentic stamp of Shakespeare's genius. Claudio's speech on the terrors of death is as eloquent as it is terrifying. It reminds us that the poet, although a Man of the Renaissance, was still haunted by the spirit of the Middle Ages.

MEASURE FOR MEASURE

Act I · Scene 1

Duke: Spirits are not finely touch'd
But to fine issues: nor nature never lends
The smallest scruple of her excellence
But, like a thrifty goddess, she determines
Herself the glory of a creditor,
Both thanks and use.
— — —

Hold therefore, Angelo:—
In our remove be thou at full ourself;
Morality and mercy in Vienna
Live in thy tongue and heart! old Escalus.
Though first in question, is thy secondary:—
Take thy commission.

Act I · Scene 2

First gentleman: There's not a soldier of us all that, in
the thanksgiving before meat, do relish the petition well
that prays for peace.

Lucio: He was ever precise in promise-keeping.

MEASURE FOR MEASURE

Act I · Scene 3

Claudio: *Our natures do pursue,—*
Like rats that ravin down their proper bane,—
A thirsty evil, and when we drink we die.

Claudio: Or whether that the body public be
A horse whereon the governor doth ride,

Act I · Scene 5

Lucio: A man whose blood
Is very snow-broth; one who never feels
The wanton stings and motions of the sense.
But doth rebate and blunt his natural edge
With profits of the mind, study, and fast.

Lucio: Our doubts are traitors,
And make us lose the good we oft might win,
By fearing to attempt.

MEASURE FOR MEASURE

Act II · Scene 1

Angelo: We must not make a scarecrow of the law,
Setting it up to fear the birds of prey,
And let it keep one shape, till custom make it
Their perch, and not their terror.
Escalus: *Ay, but yet*
Let us be keen, and rather cut a little
Than fall and bruise to death.

Angelo: 'Tis one thing to be tempted, Escalus,
Another thing to fall.

Angelo: What's open made to justice,
That justice seizes.

Angelo: The jewel that we find, we stoop and take't,
Because we see it; but what we do not see
We tread upon, and never think of it.

MEASURE FOR MEASURE

Act II · Scene 1

Escalus: Well, heaven forgive him! And forgive us all!
Some rise by sin, and some by virtue fall:
Some run from brakes of vice, and answer none;
And some condemnéd for a fault alone.

Escalus: Mercy is not itself, that oft looks so,
Pardon is still the nurse of second woe:
But yet, — poor Claudio, — There's no remedy.

Act II · Scene 2

Isabella: Too late! Why, no; I, that do speak a word,
May call it back again. Well, believe this,
No ceremony that to great ones 'longs,
Not the king's crown nor the deputed sword,
The marshal's truncheon nor the judge's robe,
Become them with one half so so good a grace
As mercy does

MEASURE FOR MEASURE

Act II · Scene 2

Isabella: O, it is excellent
To have a giant's strength, but it is tyrannous
To use it like a giant.

Isabella: But man, proud man!
Dress'd in a little brief authority, —
Most ignorant of what he's most assured,
His glassy essence, — like an angry ape,
Plays such fantastic tricks before high heaven
As make the angels weep;

Isabella: We cannot weigh our brother with ourself:
Great men may jest with saints; 'tis wit in them.
But, in the less, foul profanation.

MEASURE FOR MEASURE

Act II · Scene 4

Angelo: *O heavens!*
Why does my blood thus muster to my heart,
Making both it unable for itself
And dispossessing all my other parts
Of necessary fitness?
So play the foolish throngs with one that swoons;
Come all to help him, and so stop the air
By which he should revive.

Isabella: O, pardon me, my lord; it oft falls out,
To have what we would have, we speak not what we
mean:

Act III · Scene 1

Duke: *Thou art death's fool;*
For him thou labour'st by thy flight to shun,
And yet runn'st toward him still.

— — —

Thy best of rest is sleep,
And that thou oft provok'st; yet grossly fear'st
Thy death, which is no more.

MEASURE FOR MEASURE

Act III · Scene 1

Isabella: Darest thou die?
The sense of death is most in apprehension;
And the poor beetle that we tread upon,
In corporal sufferance finds a pang as great
As when a giant dies.

Claudio: If I must die, I will encounter darkness as
*   a bride,*
And hug it in my arms.

Claudio: Ay, but to die, and go we know not where;
To lie in cold obstruction, and to rot;
This sensible warm motion to become
A kneaded clod; and the delighted spirit
To bathe in fiery floods or to reside
In thrilling regions of thick-ribbed ice;
To be imprison'd in the viewless winds,
And blown with restless violence round about
The pendent world; or to be worse than worst
Of those that lawless and incertain thoughts
Imagine howling! — 'tis too horrible!
The weariest and most loathed worldly life
That age, ache, penury, and imprisonment
Can lay on nature is a paradise
To what we fear of death.

Claudio: The miserable have no other medicine
But only hope:

MEASURE FOR MEASURE

Act III · Scene 2

A boy singing: *Take, O take those lips away,*
That so sweetly were forsworn;
And those eyes, the break of day,
Lights that do mislead the morn:
But my kisses bring again,
Bring again;
Seals of love, but seal'd in vain,
Sealed in vain.

Act IV · Scene 2

Duke: O, death's a great disguiser,

Act V · Scene 1

Mariana: They say, best men are moulded out of
faults:
And, for the most, become much more the better
For being a little bad: so may my husband.

MUCH ADO ABOUT NOTHING

In *Love's Labour's Lost* Shakespeare had already portrayed the unending warfare between Man and Woman; but, whereas in the earlier play it takes the form of an elaborate courtly tournament, in *Much Ado About Nothing* it becomes a savage individual conflict. Benedick and Beatrice are passionate adversaries, whose amorous dissension only reaches its end when Benedick seizes Beatrice in his arms and "stops her mouth" with a fierce, impatient kiss. Meanwhile they rage eloquently both against one another and against their own emotions. Beatrice cannot forgive herself for loving; Benedick's passion almost turns to hatred; and the resultant dialogue, with its rapid thrust and parry, recalls the elegant expertise of an Elizabethan fencing-match. Misogyny, a theme that often recurs throughout sixteenth- and seventeenth-century literature, seems to have originated in the social conditions of the age. The country was ruled by a terrifying matriarch; ladies of the upper classes were often powerful and highly educated; and, according to a continental proverb, England was "the Hell of horses, the Purgatory of servants, and the Paradise of Women". Rebels like Berowne and Benedick boldly put the case for Man. But Shakespeare was a cynic as well as a realist; and he knows that they are fighting a battle they are bound to lose. *Much Ado About Nothing* was produced in 1598 or 1599, after *A Midsummer Night's Dream* and *The Merchant of Venice*. The part of Dogberry, the comic constable, whom Shakespeare is said to have modelled on an actual character whom he had encountered between Stratford and London, was apparently written for the famous actor William Kempe.

MUCH ADO ABOUT NOTHING

Act I · Scene 1

Leonato: How much better is it to weep at joy than to joy at weeping?

Beatrice: — so that if he have wit enough to keep himself warm, let him bear it for a difference between himself and his horse; for it is all the wealth that he hath left, to be known a reasonable creature.

Don Pedro: You embrace your charge too willingly — I think this is your daughter.
Leonato: Her mother hath many times told me so.
Benedick: Were you in doubt sir, that you ask'd her?
Leonato: Signior Benedick, no; for then were you a child.

Much Ado About Nothing   Act IV. Scene 2.

Dogberry: "I am a wise fellow . . ."

MUCH ADO ABOUT NOTHING

Act I · Scene 1

Claudio: — I looked upon her with a soldier's eye,
That lik'd, but had a rougher task in hand
Than to drive liking to the name of love:
But now I am return'd, and that war-thoughts,
Have left their places vacant, in their rooms
Come thronging soft and delicate desires.
All prompting me how fair young Hero is.

MUCH ADO ABOUT NOTHING

Act I · Scene 3

*Don John: I cannot hide what I am: I must be sad
when I have cause, and smile at no man's jest; eat
when I have stomach, and wait for no man's leisure;
sleep when I am drowsy, and tend on no man's
business; laugh when I am merry, and claw no man
in his humour.*

*Conrade: You have of late stood out against your
brother, and he hath ta'en you newly into his grace,
where it is impossible you should take true root but by
the fair weather that you make yourself: it is needful
that you frame the season for your own harvest.*

MUCH ADO ABOUT NOTHING

Act II · Scene 1

*Beatrice: Just, if he send me no husband; for the
which blessing I am at him upon my knees every
morning and evening. Lord! I could not endure a
husband with a beard on his face: I had rather lie in
the woollen.*

*Claudio: 'Tis certain so: — the prince woos for himself.
Friendship is constant in all other things.
Save in the office and affairs of love:*

Don Pedro: Speak low, if you speak love.

*Claudio: Therefore, all hearts in love use their own
     tongues:
Let every eye negotiate for itself,
And trust no agent: for beauty is a witch,
Against whose charms faith melteth into blood.*

*Claudio: Silence is the perfectest herald of joy: I were
but little happy if I could say how much.*

*Beatrice: But then there was a star danced, and under
that was I born.*

MUCH ADO ABOUT NOTHING

Act II · Scene 1

Claudio: Time goes on crutches till love have all his rites.

Benedick: O, she misused me past the endurance of a block; an oak with but one green leaf on it would have answered her.

Act II · Scene 3

Benedick: But till all graces be in one woman, one woman shall not come in my grace. Rich she shall be, that's certain; Wise, or I'll none; virtuous, or I'll never cheapen her; fair, or I'll never look on her; mild, or come not near me;

Balthazar: Sigh no more, ladies, sigh no more;
Men were deceivers ever;
One foot in sea and one on shore,
To one thing constant never;
Then sigh not so,
But let them go,
And be you blithe and bonny;

MUCH ADO ABOUT NOTHING

Act III · Scene 1

*Hero: My talk to thee must be how Benedick
Is sick in love with Beatrice. Of this matter
Is little Cupid's crafty arrow made,
That only wounds by hearsay.*

*Hero: One doth not know
How much an ill word may empoison liking.*

*Hero: If it prove so, then loving goes by haps:
Some Cupid kills with arrows, some with traps,*

Act III · Scene 2

*Benedick: Well, every one can master a grief but he
that has it.*

Act IV · Scene 1

*Claudio: Would you not swear,
All you that see her, that she were a maid,
By these exterior shows? But she is none;
She knows the heat of a luxurious bed;
Her blush is guiltiness, not modesty.*

*Claudio: You seem to me as Dian in her orb,
As chaste as is the bud ere it be blown;
But you are more intemperate in your blood
Than Venus, or those pamper'd animals
That rage in savage sensuality.*

MUCH ADO ABOUT NOTHING

Act IV · Scene 1

Leonato: But mine and mine I lov'd, and mine I
*   prais'd,*
And mine that I was proud on; mine so much
That I myself was to myself not mine,
Valuing of her; why she — O she is fall'n
Into a pit of ink, that the wide sea
Hath drops too few to wash her clean again.

Friar Francis: For it so falls out
That what we have we prize not to the worth
Whiles we enjoy it; but being lack'd and lost,
Why, then we rack the value; then we find
The virtue that possession would not show us
Whiles it was ours.

Leonato: Being that I flow in grief
The smallest twine may lead me.

Act IV · Scene 2

Dogberry: Dost thou not suspect my place?
Dost thou not suspect my years? —
O that he were here to write me down an ass!

MUCH ADO ABOUT NOTHING

Act V · Scene 1

Leonato: *For, brother, men*
Can counsel and speak comfort to that grief
Which they themselves not feel; but, tasting it,
Their counsel turns to passion, which before
Would give preceptial medicine to rage,
Fetter strong madness in a silken thread,
Charm ache with air and agony with words:

Claudio: Wilt thou use thy wit?
Benedick: It is in my scabbard; shall I draw it?
Don Pedro: Dost thou wear thy wit by thy side?
Claudio: Never any did so, though very many have
   been beside their wit. —

Don Pedro: What a pretty thing man is when he goes
in his doublet and hose, and leaves off his wit!

Act V · Scene 2

Beatrice: It appears not in this confession; there's not
one wise man among twenty that will praise himself.

Benedick: An old, an old instance, Beatrice, that lived
in time of good neighbours: if a man do not erect in this
age his own tomb ere he dies, he shall live no longer in
monument than the bell rings and the widow weeps.

Love's Labour's Lost · Act V. Scene I.

Song: "Spring".

LOVE'S LABOUR'S LOST

Early in 1593, an outbreak of plague closed the London play-houses. Shakespeare, no doubt, retired to the country; and about this time he wrote a poetic diversion, *Love's Labour's Lost*, which seems to have been intended for a private audience. That audience may well have been composed of Lord Southampton and his friends; and Shakespeare's comedy is packed with allusions that only they would have fully understood. Its tone is sophisticated and fashionable, more likely to amuse an aristocratic côterie than to delight the London "groundlings". The scene is laid at the French Court; the characters have French — or travesties of French — names; and the subject is the war between Man and Woman. Ferdinand, King of Navarre, and his courtiers, Biron, Dumain and Longaville, have determined to retire from feminine society; but they are pursued, and finally overcome, by the Princess of France and her resourceful ladies. Biron puts the case against Woman with tremendous eloquence and poetic fire; but Biron also pays a tribute to Love that finds an honoured place in all Shakespearian anthologies. Private jokes and contemporary references abound. Sir Walter Ralegh was Southampton's bitterest foe; and the poet tilts at Ralegh's scientific interests and his learned circle, the so-called "School of Night". *Love's Labour's Lost* is an unequal play; and some of the finest passages may have been added when the first Quarto edition, advertised as "newly corrected and augmented", made its appearance in 1598.

LOVE'S LABOUR'S LOST

Act I · Scene 1

King of Navarre: Let fame, that all hunt after in their lives,
Live register'd upon our brazen tombs,
And then grace us in the disgrace of death — — —
Therefore, brave conquerors, — for so you are —
That war against your own affections
And the huge army of the world's desires, —
Our late edict shall strongly stand in force:
Navarre shall be the wonder of the world;
Our court shall be a little academe,
Still and contemplative in living art.

Longaville: I am resolv'd; 'tis but at three years' fast;
The mind shall banquet though the body pine:
Fat paunches have lean pates; and dainty bits
Make rich the ribs, but bankrupt quite the wits.

Biron: Study is like the heaven's glorious sun,
That will not be deep-search'd with saucy looks;
Small have continual plodders ever won,
Save base authority from other's books.

Biron: These earthly godfathers of heaven's lights,
That gave a name to every fixed star,
Have no more profit of their shining nights
Than those that walk and wot not what they are.

LOVE'S LABOUR'S LOST

Act I · Scene 1

Biron: Why should proud summer boast,
Before the birds have any cause to sing?
Why should I joy in an abortive birth?
At Christmas I no more desire a rose,,
Than wish a snow in May's new-fangled earth,
But like of each thing that in season grows.

King: Our court, you know, is haunted
With a refined traveller of Spain,
A man in all the world's new fashion planted,
That hath a mint of phrases in his brain;
One whom the music of his own vain tongue
Doth ravish like enchanting harmony,
A man of complements, whom right and wrong
Have chose as umpire of their mutiny.

Act II · Scene 1

Princess: Good lord Boyet, my beauty though but
        mean,
Needs not the painted flourish of your praise:
Beauty is bought by judgment of the eye,
Not utter'd by base sale of chapmen's tongues;
I am less proud to hear you tell my worth
Than you much willing to be counted wise
In spending your wit in the praise of mine.

LOVE'S LABOUR'S LOST

Act III · Scene 1

Princess: *Nay, never paint me now;*
Where fair is not, praise cannot mend the brow.

Princess: And, out of question, so it is sometimes, —
Glory grows guilty of detested crimes;
When, for fame's sake, for praise, an outward part,
We bend to that the working of the heart:

Biron: What! I! I love! I sue! I seek a wife!
A woman, that is like a German clock,
Still a-repairing; ever out of frame;
And never going aright, being a watch,
But being watch'd that it may still go right!
Nay, to be perjur'd, which is worst of all;
And, among three, to love the worst of all;
A whitely wanton with a velvet brow,
With two pitch balls stuck in her face for eyes;
Ay, and, by heaven, one that will do the deed,
Though Argus were her eunuch and her guard:

Act IV · Scene 1

Biron: A lover's eyes will gaze an eagle blind;
A lover's ear will hear the lowest sound,
When the suspicious head of theft is stopp'd;
Love's feeling is more soft and sensible
Than are the tender horns of cockled snails;

LOVE'S LABOUR'S LOST

Act IV · Scene 3

Biron: Once more I'll mark how love can vary wit.

Biron: For where is any author in the world
Teaches such beauty as a woman's eye?
Learning is but an adjunct to ourself
And where we are our learning likewise is:
Then when ourselves we see in ladies' eyes
Do we not likewise see our learning there.

Biron: But love, first learned in a lady's eyes
Lives not alone immured in the brain,
But, with the motion of all elements,
Courses as swift as thought in every power,

Act V · Scene 2

Katharine: A light heart lives long.

Princess: We are wise girls to mock our lovers so.

Princess: None are so surely caught, when they are
catch'd,
As wit turn'd fool: folly, in wisdom hatch'd,
Hath wisdom's warrant, and the help of school,
And wit's own grace to grace a learned fool.

A MIDSUMMER NIGHT'S DREAM

Many of Shakespeare's plays, both tragedies and comedies, were written either for performance at Court or to grace some magnificent social occasion that the Queen herself attended. So it was with *A Midsummer Night's Dream*, which appears to have been composed for a fashionable wedding held in January 1595. That the Queen was present among the audience is suggested by an elaborately flattering allusion; Elizabeth, of course, is the "fair vestal", the "imperial votaress", at whom Cupid vainly directs his arrow. The fairy kingdom played an important rôle in the mythology of sixteenth-century England; and Shakespeare took the story of how a man had been transformed into an ass from a popular book entitled *The Discoverie of Witchcraft*. But to his conception of the dream itself he gave a specially Shakespearian colouring. Human life consists of a series of dreams, one enclosed within another — dreams of love, dreams of pleasure, dreams of social consequence and royal state. His personages stray through a forest of illusions, meeting and parting and mistaking their way; until day dawns and the illusory pageant dissolves. Shakespeare composed his work on several different planes. There are Oberon and Titania, and King Theseus and Queen Hippolyta, counterparts of the real sovereign seated opposite; the collection of wandering lovers, who represent the married couple; finally, the ridiculous rustics, actors in a play-inside-a-play. Shakespeare treats these well-meaning tradesmen with a somewhat cruel condescension; he parodies their misuse of the English language and their awkward attempts at self-improvement. The Elizabethan Age, like the Victorian, was deeply interested in education; popular textbooks were widely circulated; and the garrulous, self-taught artisan must have been a very common type.

A MIDSUMMER NIGHT'S DREAM

Act I · Scene 1

*Hippolyta: Four days will quickly steep themselves
        in nights;
Four nights will quickly dream away the time;
And then the moon, like to a silver bow
New bent in heaven, shall behold the night
Of our solemnities.*

*Theseus: Thrice blessed they that master so their
        blood
To undergo such maiden pilgrimage:
But earthlier happy is the rose distill'd,
Than that which, withering on the virgin thorn,
Grows, lives, and dies in single blessedness.*

*Lysander: Or, if there were a sympathy in choice,
War, death, or sickness, did lay siege to it,
Making it momentary as a sound,
Swift as a shadow, short as any dream;
Brief as the lightning in the collied night
That, in a spleen, unfolds both heaven and earth,
And ere a man hath power to say, Behold!
The jaws of darkness do devour it up:
So quick bright things come to confusion.*

*Hermia: By all the vows that ever man have broke,
In number more than ever women spoke; —
In that same place thou hast appointed me,
To-morrow truly will I meet with thee.
Lysander: Keep promise, love. Look here comes
        Helena.*

A Midsummer Night's Dream · Act II. Scene 2.

Oberon: "Ill met by moonlight, proud Titania."

A MIDSUMMER NIGHT'S DREAM

Act II · Scene 1

Puck: *Thou speak'st aright;*
I am that merry wanderer of the night:
I jest to Oberon, and make him smile,
When I a fat and bean-fed horse beguile,
Neighing in likeness of a filly foal:
And sometime lurk I in a gossip's bowl
In very likeness of a roasted crab.

Act II · Scene 3

First Fairy: You spotted snakes, with double tongue,
*   Thorny hedgehogs, be not seen;*
*   Newts and blind-worms do no wrong:*
*   Come not near our fairy queen:*

Lysander: Hermia, sleep thou there;
And never mayst thou come Lysander near!
For, as a surfeit of the sweetest things
The deepest loathing to the stomach brings;
Or, as the heresies that men do leave
Are hated most of those they did deceive;
So thou, my surfeit and my heresy
Of all be hated, but the most of me!

A MIDSUMMER NIGHT'S DREAM

Act II · Scene 3

Hermia: Help me Lysander, help me! do thy best
To pluck this crawling serpent from my breast!
Ah me, for pity! What a dream was here!
Lysander, look how I do quake with fear!
Methought a serpent eat my heart away,
And you sat smiling at his cruel prey. —

Act III · Scene 2

Helena: O weary night, O long and tedious night
Abate my hours! Shine comforts from the east
That I may back to Athens by daylight,
From these that my poor company detest:
And sleep, that sometime shuts up sorrow's eye,
Steal me awhile from mine own company.

Act IV · Scene 1

Bottom: Monsieur Cobweb; good monsieur, get your
weapons in your hand, and kill me a red-hipp'd
humble-bee on the top of a thistle; and, good monsieur,
bring me the honey-bag. Do not fret yourself too much in
the action, monsieur; and good monsieur, have a care the
honey-bag break not: I would be loath to have you overflown
with a honey-bag, signior.

A MIDSUMMER NIGHT'S DREAM

Act IV · Scene 1

Hippolyta: I was with Hercules and Cadmus once,
When in a wood of Crete they bay'd the bear
With hounds of Sparta; never did I hear
Such gallant chiding: for, besides the groves,
The skies, the fountains, every region near
Seem'd all one mutual cry:

Theseus: My hounds are bred out of the Spartan kind,
So flew'd, so sanded; and their heads are hung
With ears that sweep away the morning dew;
Crook-kneed and dew-lap'd like Thessalian bulls;
Slow in pursuit, but match'd in mowth like bells,
Each under each.

Theseus: I pray you all, stand up,
I know you two are rival enemies:
How comes this gentle concord in the world,
That hatred is so far from jealousy,
To sleep by hate, and fear no enmity.

Demetrius: But, my good lord, I wot not by what
        power, —
But by some power it is, — my love to Hermia
Melted as doth the snow — seems to me now
As the remembrance of an idle gawd
Which in my childhood I did dote upon:

Theseus: Egeus, I will overbear your will;
For in the temple, by and by with us,
These couples shall eternally be knit.
And, for the morning now is something worn,
Our purpos'd hunting shall be set aside.

A MIDSUMMER NIGHT'S DREAM

Act IV · Scene 1

*Demetrius: These things seem small and
      undistinguishable,
Like far-off mountains turned into clouds.
Hermia: Methinks I see these things with parted eye,
When everything seems double.*

*Bottom: The eye of man hath not heard, the ear of
man hath not seen; man's hand is not able to taste, his
tongue to conceive, nor his heart to report what my
dream was.*

Act IV · Scene 2

*Bottom: And most dear actors, eat not onions or
garlic; for we are to utter sweet breath; and I do not
doubt but to hear them say it is a sweet comedy.*

A MIDSUMMER NIGHT'S DREAM

Act V · Scene 1

Theseus: And, as imagination bodies forth
The form of things unknown, the poet's pen
Turns them to shapes, and gives to airy nothing
A local habitation and a name.
Such tricks hath strong imagination,

Theseus: Come now; what masks, what dances shall
      we have,
To wear away this long age of three hours
Between our after-supper and bed-time?

Theseus: I will hear that play;
For never anything can be amiss
When simpleness and duty tender it.
Go, bring them in: and take your places, ladies.

Hippolyta: I love not to see wretchedness o'ercharged,
And duty in his service perishing.

A MIDSUMMER NIGHT'S DREAM

Act V · Scene 1

Theseus: Our sport shall be to take what they mistake:
And what poor duty cannot do,
Noble respect takes it in might, not merit.

— — —

And in the modesty of fearful duty
I read as much as from the rattling tongue
Of saucy and audacious eloquence.

Prologue: If we offend, it is with our good will.
That you should think we come not to offend
But with good will. To show our simple skill,
That is the true beginning of our end.

Hippolyta: This is the silliest stuff that e'er I heard.

Theseus: The best in this kind are but shadows; and
the worst are no worse, if imagination amend them.

Hippolyta: It must be your imagination then, and not
theirs.

Theseus: If we imagine no worse of them than they of
themselves, they may pass for excellent men.

Demetrius: Well roar'd lion.
Theseus: Well run, Thisbe.

A MIDSUMMER NIGHT'S DREAM

Act V · Scene 2

Puck: Now the hungry lion roars,
And the wolf behowls the moon;
Whilst the heavy ploughman snores,
All with weary task fordone.

Puck: If we shadows have offended,
Think but this — and all is mended —
That you have but slumber'd here
While these visions did appear.
And this weak and idle theme,
No more yielding but a dream,

The Merchant of Venice · Act V. Scene 1.

*Lorenzo: "Here will we sit, and let the sounds of music creep
in our ears . . ."*

THE MERCHANT OF VENICE

The main plot of *The Merchant of Venice*, which was probably composed about the same time as *A Midsummer Night's Dream*, owed much of its bias to contemporary history. In 1594 the Queen's physician, a learned Portuguese Jew named Dr. Lopez, was accused of having attempted to poison her and of being attached to the Spanish secret service. Although William Cecil, the Queen's chief minister, did his best to defend this faithful servant, Essex, the royal favourite, insisted upon Lopez's guilt; and, still protesting his innocence, he met the hideous death reserved for traitors. Shakespeare's audience were likely to welcome a play that contained a Jewish villain; and the dramatist obliged by producing Shylock, a rôle in which the celebrated actor Burbage is said to have given one of his most remarkable performances. While he was creating his villain, however, Shakespeare's genius suddenly took control; and Shylock began to dominate the play and assume an air of genuine tragic dignity. Beside the persecuted Jew, his Christian antagonists seem trivial and insignificant characters. Perhaps the dramatist, remarked Heinrich Heine, "had in mind to create . . . a trained werewolf, a loathsome fabulous monster thirsting for blood . . . But the genius of the poet, the universal spirit that inspires him, is always above his individual will", and, whereas his fellow personages merely amuse us, he alone commands our deepest sympathies. Apart from its dramatic interest, the play has an exquisite lyrical framework; and the famous exchange between Lorenzo and Jessica, in the moonlit gardens of Belmont, is among the loveliest passages that Shakespeare ever wrote.

THE MERCHANT OF VENICE

Act I · Scene 1

Antonio: In sooth, I know not why I am so sad:
It wearies me; you say it wearies you;
But how I caught it, found it, or came by it,
What stuff 'tis made of, whereof it is born,
I am to learn;
And such a want-wit sadness makes of me
That I have much ado to know myself.

Antonio: Believe me, no: I thank my fortune for it,
My ventures are not in one bottom trusted,
Nor to one place; nor is my whole estate
Upon the fortune of this present year:
Therefore my merchandise makes me not sad.

Gratiano: You look not well, Signior Antonio;
You have too much respect upon the world:
They lose it that do buy it with much care.

Antonio: I hold the world but as the world, Gratiano —
A stage, where every man must play a part,
And mine a sad one.

THE MERCHANT OF VENICE

Act I · Scene 1

Gratiano: Let me play the fool:
With mirth and laughter let old wrinkles come;
And let my liver rather heat with wine
Than my heart cool with mortifying groans.

Gratiano: But fish not, with this melancholy bait,
For this fool's gudgeon, this opinion.

Bassanio: Gratiano speaks an infinite deal of nothing,
more than any man in all Venice. His reasons are as
two grains of wheat hid in two bushels of chaff: you
shall seek all day ere you find them; and, when you
have them, they are not worth the search.

Act I · Scene 2

Nerissa: It is no mean happiness, therefore, to be
seated in the mean: superfluity comes sooner by white
hairs, but competency lives longer.

Portia: But this reasoning is not in the fashion to
choose me a husband: — O me, the world "choose"!
I may neither choose whom I would, nor refuse whom
I dislike; so is the will of a living daughter curb'd by
the will of a dead father.

THE MERCHANT OF VENICE

Act I · Scene 2

*Portia: I fear he will prove the weeping philosopher
when he grows old, being so full of unmannerly
sadness in his youth..I had rather be married to a
death's head with a bone in his mouth than to either of
these. God defend me from these two!*

*Nerissa: How like you the young German, the Duke
of Saxony's nephew?*
*Portia: Very vilely in the morning when he is sober;
and most vilely in the afternoon when he is drunk:
when he is best he is a little worse than a man; and
when he is worst, he is a little better than a beast.*

Act I · Scene 3

*Antonio: Mark you this, Bassanio,
The devil can cite scripture for his purpose.*

*Antonio: If thou wilt lend this money, lend it not
As to thy friends, (for when did friendship take
A breed for barren metal of his friend?)
But lend it rather to thine enemy,
Who if he breaks, thou mayst with better face
Exact the penalty.*

THE MERCHANT OF VENICE

Act I · Scene 3

Shylock: Go with me to a notary, seal me there
Your single bond; and, in a merry sport,
If you repay me not on such a day,
In such a place, such a sum or sums as are
Express'd in the condition, let the forfeit
Be nominated for an equal pound
Of your fair flesh, to be cut off and taken
In what part of your body pleaseth me.

Act II · Scene 1

Prince of Morocco: Mislike me not for my
complexion,
The shadow'd livery of the burnish'd sun,
To whom I am a neighbour and near bred.
Bring me the fairest creature northward born,
Where Phoebus' fire scarce thaws the icicles.
And let us make incision for your love,
To prove whose blood is reddest, his or mine.

Portia: But, if my father had not scanted me,
And hedg'd me by his wit, to yield myself
His wife who wins me by that means I told you,
Yourself, renowned prince, then stood as fair
As any comer I have look'd on yet
For my affection.

THE MERCHANT OF VENICE

Act II · Scene 1

Prince of Morocco: *By this scimitar, —*
That slew the Sophy, and a Persian prince
That won three fields of Sultan Solyman, —
I would outstare the sternest eyes that look,
Outbrave the heart most daring on the earth,
Pluck the young sucking cubs from the she-bear,
Yea, mock the lion when he roars for prey,
To win the lady. But, alas the while!

Act II · Scene 2

Launcelot Gobbo: The old proverb is very well parted
between my master, Shylock, and you, sir; you have
the grace of God, sir, and he hath enough.

Bassanio: *But hear thee, Gratiano;*
Thou art too wild, too rude and bold of voice, —
Parts that become thee happily enough,
And in such eyes as ours appear not faults;
But where thou art not known, why, there they show
Something too liberal. Prithee, take pain
To allay with some cold drops of modesty
Thy skipping spirit.

Act II · Scene 3

Jessica: Alack what heinous sin is it in me
To be asham'd to be my father's child!
But though I am a daughter to his blood,
I am not to his manners.

THE MERCHANT OF VENICE

Act II · Scene 6

Gratiano: Where is the horse that doth untread again
His tedious measures with the unbated fire
That he did pace them first? All things that are,
Are with more spirit chas'd than enjoy'd.

Lorenzo: So are you, sweet,
Even in the lovely garnish of a boy.
But come at once;
For the close night doth play the runaway,
And we are stay'd for at Bassanio's feast.

Act II · Scene 7

Prince of Morocco: What says this leaden casket? —
"Who chooseth me must give and hazard all he hath"
Must give — for what? for lead? hazard for lead?
This casket threatens: men that hazard all
Do it in hope of fair advantages.

Prince of Morocco: Why that's the lady: all the world
*   desires her;*
From the four corners of the earth they come,
To kiss this shrine, this mortal breathing saint;
The Hyrcanian deserts and the vasty wilds
Of wide Arabia are as throughfares now
For princes to come view fair Portia.

THE MERCHANT OF VENICE

Act II · Scene 9

*Prince of Arragon: I will not choose what many men
    desire,
Because I will not jump with common spirits,
And rank me with the barbarous multitudes.
Why, then to thee, thou silver treasure-house;
Tell me once more what title thou dost bear;
"Who chooseth me shall get as much as he deserves":*

*Portia: To offend, and judge are distinct offices,
And of opposed natures.*

*Nerissa: The ancient saying is no heresy, —
Hanging and wiving goes by destiny.*

Act III · Scene 1

*Shylock: I am a Jew. Hath not a Jew eyes? hath not a
Jew hands, organs, dimensions, senses, affections
passions? fed with the same food, hurt with the same
weapons, subject to the same diseases, heal'd by the
same means, warm'd and cool'd by the same winter
and summer as a Christian? If you prick us, do we
not bleed? if you tickle us, do we not laugh? if you
poison us, do we not die? and if you wrong us, shall
we not revenge? If we are like you in the rest, we will
resemble you in that.*

THE MERCHANT OF VENICE

Act III · Scene 2

Portia: And yet a maiden hath no tongue but thought —
I would detain you here some month or two
Before you venture for me. I could teach you
How to choose right, but then I am forsworn;
So I will never be; so may you miss me:

Portia: How all the other passions fleet to air,
As doubtful thoughts, and rash-embrac'd despair,
And shudd'ring fear, and green-ey'd jealousy!
O love, be moderate, allay thy ecstasy,
In measure rain thy joy,

Portia: But the full sum of me
Is sum of something, which, to term in gross,
Is an unlesson'd girl, unschool'd, unpractis'd:
Happy in this, she is not yet so old
But she may learn; and happier than this,
She is not bred so dull but she can learn;

Portia: There are some shrewd contents in yond same
*   paper,*
That steals the colour from Bassanio's cheek:
Some dear friend dead; else nothing in the world
Could turn so much the constitution
Of any constant man. What, worse and worse! —
With leave Bassanio; I am half yourself
And I must freely have the half of any thing
That this same paper brings you.

THE MERCHANT OF VENICE

Act III · Scene 2

Bassanio: The dearest friend to me, the kindest man.
The best-condition'd and unwearied spirit
In doing courtesies: and one in whom
The ancient Roman honour more appears
Than any that draws breath in Italy.

Portia: What no more?
Pay him six thousand, and deface the bond;
Double six thousand, and then treble that
Before a friend of this description
Shall lose a hair through Bassanio's fault.
First go with me to church and call me wife
And then away to Venice to your friend
For never shall you lie by Portia's side
With an unquiet soul.

Act III · Scene 3

Shylock: I'll have my bond, I will not hear thee speak:
I'll have my bond; and therefore speak no more.
I'll not be made a soft and dull-eyed fool,
To shake the head, relent, and sigh, and yield
To Christian intercessors. Follow not;
I'll have no speaking: I will have my bond.

THE MERCHANT OF VENICE

Act III · Scene 4

Portia: *In companions*
That do converse and waste the time together,
Whose souls do bear an equal yoke of love,
There must be needs a like proportion
Of lineaments, of manners, and of spirit,

Portia: *Now, Balthazar,*
As I have ever found thee honest, true,
So let me find thee still. Take this same letter,
And use thou all the endeavour of a man
In speed to Padua; see thou render this
Into my cousin's hand, Doctor Bellario;
And look, what notes and garments he doth give thee,
Bring them, I pray thee, with imagin'd speed
Unto the tranect, to the common ferry
Which trades to Venice. Waste no time in words
But get thee gone.

Act III · Scene 5

Lorenzo: How every fool can play upon the word!
I think the best grace of wit will shortly turn into
silence, and discourse grow commendable in none only
but parrots.

THE MERCHANT OF VENICE

Act IV · Scene 1

Bassanio: Do all men kill the things they do not love?
Shylock: Hates any man the thing he would not kill?
Bassanio: Every offence is not a hate at first.
Shylock: What! would'st thou have a serpent sting
thee twice?

Shylock: What judgment shall I dread, doing no wrong?
You have among you many a purchas'd slave,
Which, like your asses, and your dogs and mules,
You use in abject and in slavish parts,
Because you bought them. — Shall I say to you,
Let them be free, marry them to your heirs?

Clerk [reads]: I beseech you, let his lack of years be
no impediment to let him lack a reverend estimation;
for I never knew so young a body with so old a head.
I leave him to your gracious acceptance, whose trial
shall better publish his commendation.

Portia: The quality of mery is not strain'd;
It droppeth as the gentle rain from heaven
Upon the place beneath: it is twice bless'd;
It blesseth him that gives and him that takes:

THE MERCHANT OF VENICE

Act IV · Scene 1

Portia: Tarry a little; there is something else.
This bond doth give thee here no jot of blood,
The words expressly are, "a pound of flesh";
Take then thy bond, take thou thy pound of flesh;
But in the cutting it, if thou dost shed
One drop of Christian blood, thy lands and goods
Are, by the laws of Venice, confiscate
Unto the state of Venice.

Bassanio: Good sir, this ring was given me by my wife;
And, when she put it on, she made me vow
That I should neither sell nor give nor lose it.

Portia: That 'scuse serves many men to save their gifts.
An if your wife be not a mad woman,
And know how well I have deserved this ring,
She would not hold out enemy for ever
For giving it to me. Well, peace be with you!

THE MERCHANT OF VENICE

Act V · Scene 1

Lorenzo: *In such a night*
Did Jessica steal from the wealthy Jew
And, with an unthrift love, did run from Venice
As far as Belmont.

Jessica: *In such a night*
Did young Lorenzo swear he lov'd her well. —
Stealing her soul with many vows of faith,
And ne'er a true one.

Lorenzo: How sweet the moonlight sleeps upon this
      bank!
Here will we sit, and let the sounds of music
Creep in our ears; soft stillness and the night
Become the touches of sweet harmony.
Sit, Jessica. Look how the floor of heaven
Is thick inlaid with patines of bright gold;
There's not the smallest orb which thou behold'st
But in his motion like an angel sings,
Still quiring to the young-ey'd cherubims:
Such harmony is in immortal souls;
But, whilst this muddy vesture of decay
Doth grossly close it in, we cannot hear it.

Portia: That the light we see is burning in my hall:
How far that little candle throws his beams!
So shines a good deed in a naughty world.

THE MERCHANT OF VENICE

Act V · Scene 1

Portia: The crow doth sing as sweetly as the lark
When neither is attended; and, I think,
The nightingale, if she should sing by day,
When every goose is cackling, would be thought
No better a musician than the wren.

Portia: Let me give light, but let me not be light;
For a light wife doth make a heavy husband,
And never be Bassanio so for me;

Portia: A quarrel, ho, already! What's the matter?
Gratiano: About a hoop of gold, a paltry ring
That she did give to me; whose poesy was,
For all the world, like cutler's poetry
Upon a knife, "Love me, and leave me not".

Portia: I gave my love a ring, and made him swear
Never to part with it; and here he stands, —
I dare be sworn for him, he would not leave it,
Nor pluck it from his fingers, for the wealth
That the world masters. Now in faith, Gratiano,
You give your wife too unkind a cause of grief:
An 'twere to me, I should be mad at it.

Bassanio: Sweet Portia,
If you did know to whom I gave the ring,
And would conceive for what I gave the ring.
And how unwillingly I left the ring,
When naught would be accepted but the ring,
You would abate the strength of your displeasure.

AS YOU LIKE IT

First produced in 1599 or 1600, *As You Like It* is, without a doubt, Shakespeare's most popular romantic comedy. The part of Rosalind, wrote Bernard Shaw, is "to the actress what Hamlet is to the actor — a part in which, reasonable presentability being granted, failure is hardly possible". But, on the subject of Rosalind herself, he observed that she was "not a complete human being: she is simply an extension into five acts of the most . . . delightful five minutes" in a charming woman's life. Recent critics have done their best to equip the story with a moral burden, suggesting that it presents a vision of the happiness that may arise from "personally satisfying, humanely poised and socially accepted love". This view of the play is extremely difficult to accept. *As You Like It* is a poetic *capriccio,* a fantasy in which Shakespeare's boy-actors could display their adolescent graces. Rosalind's attitude towards love and marriage is very often lightly mocking. As for the gloomy philosopher Jaques, he is a type rather than an individual — the "humorous" man who occupies so important a place in Elizabethan literature, the "humour" that dominates Jaques being melancholy or the black bile. Incidentally, his famous speech concerning the Ages of Man is the elaboration of a traditional theme known to every sixteenth-century rhetorician. But the atmosphere of the whole play is extraordinarily gay and carefree. Again Shakespeare, when he wrote it, was remembering his own youth, and named the Forest of Arden after an ancient stretch of woodlands that lies a little to the north of Stratford. There his characters "fleet the time carelessly, as they did in the golden world".

AS YOU LIKE IT

Act I · Scene 1

*Touchstone: The more pity, that fools may not speak
wisely that wise men do foolishly.
Celia: By my troth, thou sayest true; for since the
little wit that fools have was silenced, the little foolery
that wise men have makes a great show.*

Act II · Scene 1

*DukeSenior: Sweet are the uses of adversity
Which, like the toad, ugly and venomous,
Wears yet a precious jewel in his head;
And this our life, exempt from public haunt,
Finds tongues in trees, books in the running brooks,
Sermons in stones, and good in every thing.*

Act II · Scene 3

*Adam: Your praise is come too swiftly home before
you.
Know you not, master, to some kind of men
Their graces serve them but as enemies?
No more do yours: your virtues, gentle master,
Are sanctified and holy traitors to you,
O what a world is this, when what is comely
Envenoms him that bears it!*

As You Like It · Act II. Scene 7.

Jacques: "*O that I were a fool! I am ambitious for a motley coat.*"

AS YOU LIKE IT

Act II · Scene 7

Jacques: A fool, a fool! — I met a fool i' the forest,
Says very wisely, "It is ten o'clock:

— — —

"Thus we may see", quoth he, "how the world wags.
'Tis but an hour ago since it was nine;
And after one hour more 'twill be eleven;
And so, from hour to hour, we ripe and ripe;
And then, from hour to hour, we rot, and rot;
And thereby hangs a tale".

Amiens sings:
   Blow, blow, thou winter wind,
   Thou art not so unkind
    As man's ingratitude;
   Thy tooth is not so keen,
   Because thou art not seen,
    Although thy breath be rude.
Heigh-ho! sing, heigh-ho! unto the green holly:
Most friendship is feigning, most living mere folly:
   Then, heigh-ho, the holly!
   This life is most jolly.

   Freeze, freeze, thou bitter sky,
   That dost not bite so nigh
    As benefits forgot:
   Though thou the waters warp
   Thy sting is not so sharp
    As friend remember'd not.
Heigh-ho! sing, heigh-ho! unto the green holly:
Most friendship is feigning, most loving mere folly:
   Then, heigh-ho, the holly!
   This life is most jolly.

AS YOU LIKE IT

Act IV . Scene 1

Orlando: *Of a snail!*
Rosalind: Ay, of a snail; for though he comes slowly,
he carries his house on his head, — a better jointure,
I think, than you make a woman: besides, he brings
his destiny with him.

Act V · Scene 1

Rosalind: Men have died from time to time, and
worms have eaten them, but not from love.

Act V · Scene 2

Rosalind: O, I know where you are: — nay, 'tis
true: there was never anything so sudden but
the fight of two rams and Caesar's thrasonical brag
of — I came, saw, and overcame: for your brother and
my sister no sooner met, but they looked; no sooner
looked, but they loved; no sooner loved, but they
sighed; no sooner sighed, but they asked one another
the reason; no sooner knew the reason, but they
sought the remedy: and in these degrees have they
made a pair of stairs to marriage, which they will
climb incontinent, or else be incontinent before
marriage: they are in the very wrath of love, and they
will together: clubs cannot part them.

Orlando: They shall be married tomorrow; and I will
bid the duke to the nuptial. But O, how bitter a thing
it is to look into happiness through another man's
eyes!

AS YOU LIKE IT

Act V · Scene 3

Song: *It was a lover and his lass,*
  With a hey, and a ho, and a hey nonino,
  That o'er the green corn-field did pass
  In the spring time, the only pretty ring time,
  When birds do sing, hey ding a ding, ding:
  Sweet lovers love the spring.

  Between the acres of the rye,
  With a hey, and a ho, and a hey nonino,
  These pretty country folks would lie,
  In the spring time, the only pretty ring time,
  When birds do sing, hey ding a ding, ding:
  Sweet lovers love the spring.

  This carol they began that hour,
  With a hey, and a ho, and a hey nonino
  How that life was but a flower
  In the spring time, the only pretty ring time,
  When birds so sing, hey ding a ding, ding:
  Sweet lovers love the spring.

  And therefore take the present time,
  With a hey, and a ho, and a hey nonino,
  For love is crowned with the prime
  In the spring time, the only pretty ring time,
  When birds do sing, hey ding a ding, ding:
  Sweet lovers love the spring.

The Taming of the Shrew · Act II. Scene 1.

Petruchio: "Good-morrow, Kate . . ."

THE TAMING OF THE SHREW

Shakespeare's first group of comedies, *Love's Labour's Lost, The Two Gentlemen of Verona, The Comedy of Errors* and *The Taming of the Shrew* are believed all to have been written before the year 1594. Their author was still a hireling dramatist; and such dramatists, we know from the private accounts of the theatrical *entrepreneur* Philip Henslowe, having submitted a skeleton plot for the players' approval, were obliged to deliver so many sheets a day. In *The Taming of the Shrew* we certainly feel that Shakespeare was often working against time; it is a mixture of high and low comedy, of genuine humour and riotous knockabout farce. Petruchio is a fine, extravagant figure, with a poetic grasp of words and imagery; but the story of how he courts his beloved, and breaks down her proud, aggresive spirit, is conceived on a much lower level. Yet the play seems to have been written in a mood of real enjoyment; and, here as elsewhere, Shakespeare enjoyed remembering the rural background of his own youth — the chestnuts roasting beside a farmer's fire and the hazel-trees along the Warwickshire lanes:

> *Kate like the hazel-twig*
> *Is straight and slender, and as brown in hue*
> *As hazel-nuts and sweeter than the kernels.*

Shakespeare alone could have produced so vivid an impression of grace in a single, plainly-worded sentence.

THE TAMING OF THE SHREW

Induction · Scene 1

Lord: O monstrous beast! how like a swine he lies!
Grim death, how foul and loathsome is thine image!
Sirs, I will practise on this drunken man.
What think you, if he were convey'd to bed,
Wrapp'd in sweet clothes, rings put upon his fingers,
A most delicious banquet by his bed,
And brave attendants near him when he wakes. —
Would not the beggar then forget himself?

Act I · Scene 2

Hortensio: I can, Petruchio, help thee to a wife
With wealth enough, and young and beauteous;
Brought up as best becomes a gentlewoman:
Her only fault — and that is fault enough —
Is, that she is intolerable curst,
And shrewd, and forward; so beyond all measure.
That, were my state far worser than it is
I would not wed her for a mine of gold.

Act II · Scene 1

Petruchio: Why that is nothing; for I tell you, father,
I am as peremptory as she proud-minded;
And where two raging fires meet together,
They do consume the thing that feeds their fury;
Though little fire grows great with little wind,
Yet extreme gusts will blow out fire and all;
So I to her, and so she yields to me.

110

THE TAMING OF THE SHREW

Act III · Scene 1

Lucentio: Preposterous ass! that never read so far
To know the cause why music was ordain'd!
Was it not to refresh the mind of man
After his studies or his usual pain?

Act III · Scene 2

Petruchio: But where is Kate? I stay too long from her:
The morning wears, 'tis time we were at church.
Tranio: See not your bride in these unreverent robes:
Go to my chamber: put on clothes of mine.
Petruchio: Not I, believe me: thus I will visit her.
Baptista: But thus, I trust, you will not marry her
Petruchio: Good sooth, even thus; therefore ha' done
*   with words;*
To me she's married, not unto my clothes:

Act V · Scene 2

Petruchio: Marry, peace it bodes, and love,
*   and quiet life,*
An awful rule, and right supremacy;
And, to be short, what not, that's sweet and happy.

Katharina: I am asham'd that women are so simple
To offer war where they should kneel for peace,
Or seek for rule, supremacy, and sway,
When they are bound to serve, love, and obey,

All's Well That Ends Well · Act I. Scene 1.

Helena: "'Twas pretty, though a plague, to see him every hour . . ."

ALL'S WELL THAT ENDS WELL

Shakespeare's first group of comedies seem to have been written for a courtly audience; their tone is carefree and high spirited; they are concerned with the doings of handsome, well-born young men and of gaily impulsive and attractive girls. Into the later comedies — those produced after 1601 — begins to creep a very different note. They have happy endings; but, unlike earlier plays, they do not reflect a spirit of genuine happiness. Their subject is still romantic love; but Shakespeare often gives the theme an odd and disconcerting twist. *All's Well That Ends Well*, for example, which, at least in its present form, was probably written between 1601 and 1608, tells a peculiarly unpleasing story — that of a young woman who can only persuade her reluctant husband to consummate their marriage by smuggling herself into his bed when he expects another bedfellow. Coleridge, however, described Helena as one of Shakespeare's loveliest creations; and it is true that her description of her feeling for the snobbish and deceitful Bertram is a peculiarly delightful speech:

> *'Twas pretty, though a plague,*
> *To see him every hour, to sit and draw*
> *His arched brow, his hawking eye, his curls,*
> *In our heart's table; heart too capable*
> *Of every line and trick of his sweet favour . . .*

— which lends distinction and lyric grace to an otherwise somewhat unrewarding play.

ALL'S WELL THAT ENDS WELL

Act I · Scene 1

Countess: Love all, trust a few,
Do wrong to none: be able for thine enemy
Rather in power than use; and keep thy friend
Under thy own life's key:

Helen: There is no living, none,
If Bertram be away. It were all one
That I should love a bright particular star,
And think to wed it, he is so above me:
In his bright radiance and collateral light
Must I be comforted, not in his sphere.
The ambition in my love this plagues itself:
The hind that would be mated by the lion
Must die for love. 'Twas pretty, though a plague,
To see him every hour; to sit and draw
His arched brows, his hawking eye, his curls,
In our heart's table, — heart too capable
Of every line and trick of his sweet favour:
But now he's gone, and my idolatrous fancy
Must sanctify his relics.

Parolles: Besides, virginity is peevish, proud, idle,
made of self-love which is the most inhibited sin in the
canon.

Parolles: 'Tis a commodity will lose the gloss with
lying; the longer kept, the less worth: off with't while
tis vendible; answer the time of request.

ALL'S WELL THAT ENDS WELL

Act I · Scene 1

Helena: Our remedies oft in ourselves do lie
Which we ascribe to heaven: the fated sky
Gives us free scope; only doth backward pull
Our slow designs when we ourselves are dull.

Helen: Impossible be strange attempts to those
That weigh their pains in sense, and do suppose
What hath been cannot be.

Act I · Scene 3

Clown: Though honesty be no puritan, yet it will do
no hurt; it will wear the surplice of humility over the
black gown of a big heart.

Act II · Scene 1

King: And yet my heart
Will not confess he owes the malady
That doth my life besiege. Farewell, young lords;
Whether I live or die, be you the sons
Of worthy Frenchmen: let higher Italy —
Those bated that inherit but the fall
Of the last monarchy — see that you come
Not to woo honour, but to wed it,

ALL'S WELL THAT ENDS WELL

Act II · Scene 3

Parolles: A young man married is a man that's marr'd:

Act II · Scene 5

Lafeu: A good traveller is something at the latter end of a dinner;

Act III · Scene 2

Countess: I have felt so many quirks of joy and grief
That the first face of neither, on the start,
Can women me unto't.

Act IV · Scene 2

'Tis not the many oaths that makes the truth,
But the plain single vow that is vow'd true
What is not holy, that we swear not by,
But take the High'st to witness.

Act IV · Scene 3

First Lord: The web of our life is of a mingled yarn,
good and ill together;

ALL'S WELL THAT ENDS WELL

Act V · Scene 3

Countess: And I beseech your majesty to make it
Natural rebellion, done i' the blaze of youth,
When oil and fire, too strong for reason's force
O'erbears it and burns on.

The King: For we are old, and on our quick'st decrees
The inaudible and noiseless foot of time
Steals ere we can effect them.

Bertram: She knew her distance, and did angle for me,
Madding my eagerness with her restraint,
As all impediments in fancy's course
Are motives of more fancy;

Bertram:Thence it came
That she whom all men prais'd and whom myself,
Since I have lost, have lov'd, was in mine eye
The dust that did offend it.

Parolles:He did love her, sir, as a gentleman loves a
woman.
King: How is that?
Parolles: He loved her, sir, and loved her not.

Twelfth Night · Act II. Scene 3.

Malvolio: "My masters, are you mad? or what are you?"

TWELFTH NIGHT

Tolstoi wrote of Tchechov's story *The Darling* that, although the great storyteller had set out to ridicule and abuse his heroine, he had inadvertently exalted her. Such was the good fortune of many Shakespearian personages, including Shylock, Falstaff and Malvolio. All begin as villainous or ludicrous characters; each breaks away from Shakespeare's original design and moves into the centre of the stage. Thus Olivia's conceited steward soon transcends his limitations; like Shylock, he is a lonely man, mocked and ill-used by his more gregarious fellows. Elsewhere I have compared him, when he is seen "practising behaviour to his own shadow" in the garden, with Richard III, who also courts his shadow. Malvolio is an egotist, "sick of self-love"; at the same time, he is far more admirable than those two greedy and pathetic hangers-on, Sir Toby Belch and Sir Andrew Aguecheek. Malvolio, observed Charles Lamb, "is not essentially ludicrous . . . but dignified, consistent and . . . of an over-stretched morality". He represents social order and conventional virtue; and his reward is to be mistaken for a lunatic and relegated to the "hideous darkness" of a madman's cell. *Twelfth Night* was probably produced at Court, and was afterwards revived, in February, 1602, to entertain the students of the Middle Temple. The part of Clown, who winds up the performance with his haunting nonsense-song, was taken by the famous Robert Armin, the highly gifted mime who, in Shakespeare's company, succeeded that no-less celebrated William Kempe.

TWELFTH NIGHT

Act I · Scene 1

Duke: So full of shapes is fancy,
That it alone is high-fantastical.

Duke: Why, so I do, the noblest that I have:
O, when mine eyes did see Olivia first,
Methought she purg'd the air of pestilence!
That instant was I turn'd into a hart;
And my desires, like fell and cruel hounds,
E'er since pursue me.

Act I · Scene 3

Sir Toby: O, knight, thou lack'st a cup of canary:
when did I see thee so put down?
Sir Andrew Aguecheek: Never in your life, I think;
unless you see canary put me down. Methinks
sometimes I have no more wit than a Christian or an
ordinary man has; but I am a great eater of beef and,
I believe, that does harm to my wit.

TWELFTH NIGHT

Act I · Scene 5

*Clown: Let her hang me: he that is well hang'd in this
world need to fear no colours.
Maria: Make that good.
Clown: He shall see none to fear.
Maria: A good lenten answer: I can tell thee where
that saying was born of, — I fear no colours.
Clown: Where, good Mistress Mary?
Maria: In the wars; and that may you be bold to say
in your foolery.*

*Clown: Many a good hanging prevents a bad
marriage;*

*Clown: One draught above heat makes him a fool;
the second mads him; and a third drowns him.*

Act II · Scene 2

*Viola: How easy is it for the proper-false
In women's waxen hearts to set their forms!*

Viola: For, such as we are made of, such we be.

TWELFTH NIGHT

Act II · Scene 3

Clown: What is love? 'tis not hereafter;
Present mirth hath present laughter;
What's to come is still unsure:

Clown: Then come kiss me, sweet and twenty,
Youth's a stuff will not endure.

Act II · Scene 4

Duke: There is no woman's side
Can hide the beating of so strong a passion
As love doth give my heart; no woman's heart
So big, to hold so much; they lack retention.
Alas, their love may be call'd appetite. —
No motion of the liver, but the palate.

TWELFTH NIGHT

Act III · Scene 1

*Clown: And fools are as like husbands as pilchards are
to herrings, the husband's the bigger;*

*Viola: This fellow's wise enough to play the fool;
And, to do that well, craves a kind of wit:
He must observe their mood on whom he jests,
The quality of persons, and the time;*

*Olivia: O what a deal of scorn looks beautiful
In the contempt and anger of his lips!
A murd'rous guilt shows not itself more soon
Than love that would seem hid: love's night is noon.*

Act III · Scene 4

*Malvolio: Some are born great, — some achieve
greatness, — and some have greatness thrust upon them.*

TWELFTH NIGHT

Act V · Scene 1

Viola: After him I love
More than I love these eyes, more than my life,
More, by all mores, than e'er I shall love wife;

Priest: A contrast of eternal bond of love,
Confirm'd by mutual joinder of your hands,
Attested by the holy close of lips,
Strengthen'd by interchangement of your rings;
And all the ceremony of this compact
Seal'd in my function, by my testimony.

Duke: O thou dissembling cub! what will thou be
When time hath sow'd a grizzle on thy case?
Or will not else thy craft so quickly grow,
That thine own trip shall be thine overthrow?

TWELFTH NIGHT

Act V · Scene 1

Clown: When that I was and a little tiny boy,
With hey, ho, the wind and the rain,
A foolish thing was but a toy,
For the rain it raineth every day.

But when I came to man's estate,
With hey, ho, the wind and the rain,
'Gainst knave and thief men shut their gate,
For the rain it raineth every day.

But when I came, alas! to wive,
With hey, ho, the wind and the rain,
By swaggering could I never thrive,
For the rain it raineth every day.

But when I came unto my bed,
With hey, ho, the wind and the rain,
With toss-pots still had drunken head,
For the rain it raineth every day.

A great while ago the world began,
With hey, ho, the wind and the rain,
But that's all one, our play is done,
And we'll strive to please you every day.

The Winter's Tale · Act IV. Scene 3.

Perdita: ". . . daffodils, that come before the swallow dares . . ."

126

THE WINTER'S TALE

Victorian critics liked to imagine that Shakespeare, towards the end of his existence, may have enjoyed a period of Olympian calm, having at length reached the state of "serene self-possession he had sought with such persistent effort". This was the period when he wrote his last two comedies; and neither *The Tempest* nor *The Winter's Tale* suggests that the poet's mood was altogether optimistic. Just as *The Tempest* has ominous undertones, so *The Winter's Tale*, for all its beauty and gaiety, begins upon a somewhat gloomy note — as a study of violent sexual jealousy, which produces a bitter quarrel between devoted friends; while the play includes frequent references to the sorrows and uncertainties of human life. But, once the dramatist has fairly launched out into his tale, the spirit of happiness re-asserts itself; and we enter the "golden world" inhabited by Perdita and the shepherds, far off in a mysterious region near Bohemia's non-existent coast-line. The atmosphere of the comedy is that of a fairy-tale; its plot, full of romantic absurdies and diverting freaks of fancy; while Perdita is a fairy-tale heroine, whose love of flowers and skill in the dance recalls two ruling Elizabethan tastes. As attractive a creation as Miranda, with the same spontaneity and unspoiled freshness, she is less innocent or at least much more candid, and does not hesitate to speak of a flowery bank where she would hold her lover in her arms. *The Winter's Tale* was first performed during the spring or early summer of 1611. Shakespeare took the story from a novel, *Pandosto*, published in 1588 by his one-time adversary Robert Greene.

THE WINTER'S TALE

Act I · Scene 1

*Camillo: You pay a great deal too dear for what's
given freely.*

*Archidamus: Believe me, I speak as my understanding
instructs me, and as mine honesty puts it to utterance.*

*Camillo: It is a gallant child; one that, indeed,
physics the subject, makes old hearts fresh: they that
went on crutches ere he was born desire yet their life
to see him a man.*

Act I · Scene 2

*Polixenes: We were, fair queen,
Two lads that thought there was no more behind,
But such a day to-morrow as to-day,
And to be boy eternal.*

THE WINTER'S TALE

Act I · Scene 2

King Leontes: — *woman say so,*
That will say anything: but were they false
As o'er dyed blacks, as wind, as waters, — false
As dice are to be wish'd by one, that fixes
No bourn 'twixt his and mine; yet were it true
To say this boy were like me.

King Leontes: How sometimes nature will betray its
       folly,
Its tenderness, and make itself a pastime
To harden bosoms!

King Leontes: Too hot, too hot!
To mingle friendship far is mingling bloods.

King Leontes: The purity and whiteness of my sheets, —
Which to preserve is sleep; which being spotted
Is goads, thorns, nettles, tails of wasps;

Kjng Leontes: To bide upon 't, —
       thou art not honest; or
If thou inclin'st that way, thou art a coward,
Which hoxes honesty behind, restraining
From course requir'd;

THE WINTER'S TALE

Act I · Scene 2

*King Leontes: Are you so fond of your young prince
        as we
Do seem to be of ours?
Polixenes: If at home, sir,
He's all my exercise, my mirth, my matter:*

*Camillo: My gracious lord,
I may be negligent, foolish, and fearful;
In every one of these no man is free,
But that his negligence, his folly, fear,
Amongst the infinite doings of the world,
Sometime puts forth: in your affairs, my lord.
If ever I were wilful-negligent,
It was my folly; if industriously
I play'd the fool, it was my negligence,
Not weighing well the end;*

*King Leontes: Should all despair
That have revolted wives, the tenth of mankind
Would hang themselves.*

THE WINTER'S TALE

Act II · Scene 1

First Lady: Why, my sweet lord?
Mamillius: You'll kiss me hard, and speak to me as if
I were a baby still — I love you better.
Second Lady: And why so, my lord?
Mamillius: Not for because
Your brows are blacker, yet black brows they say,
Become some women best; so that there be not
Too much hair there, but in a semicircle,
Or a half-moon made with a pen.

Mamillius: A sad tale's best for winter:

Hermione: There's some ill planet reigns:
I must be patient till the heavens look
With an aspect more favourable.

THE WINTER'S TALE

Act II · Scene 1

Hermione: *Do not weep good fools;*
There is no cause: when you shall know your mistress
Has deserv'd prison, then abound in tears
As I come out: this action I now go on
Is for my better grace, Adieu, my lord;
I never wish'd to see you sorry; now
I trust I shall.

First Lord: *For her, my lord,*
I dare my life lay down, and will do't, sir.
Please you t'accept it, that the queen is spotless
I' the eyes of heaven and to you: I mean.
In this which you accuse her.

Act II · Scene 2

Emilia: She is something before her time deliver'd
Paulina: A boy?
Emilia: A daughter; and a goodly babe,
Lusty, and like to live; the queen receives
Much comfort in't; says, "My poor prisoner,
I am as innocent as you".

Paulina: The silence often of pure innocence
Persuades, when speaking fails.

THE WINTER'S TALE

Act II · Scene 3

Leontes: Nor night nor day no rest; it is but weakness
To bear the matter thus, — mere weakness. If
The cause were not in being, — part o' the cause,
She, the adultress: for the harlot king
Is quite beyond mine arm, out of the blank
And level of my brain, plot-proof; but she
I can hook to me, — say that she were gone,
Given to the fire, a moiety of my rest
Might come to me again.

Leontes: I am a feather for each wind that blows:
Shall I live on, to see this bastard kneel
And call me father? better burn it now
Than curse it then. But be it, let it live
It shall not neither.

Antigonus: I swear to do this, though a present death
Had been more merciful — Come on poor babe:
Some powerful spirit instruct the kites and ravens
To be thy nurse! Wolves and bears they say,
Casting their savageness aside have done
Like offices of pity.

THE WINTER'S TALE

Act III · Scene 1

Cleomenes: The climate's delicate; the air most sweet:
Fertile the isle; the temple much surpassing
The common praise it bears.

Act III · Scene 2

Hermione: Sir, spare your threats:
The bug which you would fright me with, I seek.
To me can life be no commodity:
The crown and comfort of my life, your favour,
I do give lost; for I do feel it gone,
But know not how it went:

Paulina: What's gone, and what's past help,
Should be past grief:

Act III · Scene 3

Antigonus: The storm begins: — poor wretch
That for my mother's fault, art thus expos'd
To loss and what may follow. — Weep I cannot,
But my heart bleeds: and most accurst am I
To be by oath enjoin'd to this.

THE WINTER'S TALE

Act III · Scene 3

Shepherd: I would there were no age between ten and three-and-twenty, or that youth would sleep out the rest; for there is nothing in the between but getting wenches with child, wronging the ancientary, stealing, fighting — Hark you now! — Would any but these boil'd brains of nineteen and two-and-twenty hunt this weather?

Act IV · Scene 2

Autolycus (singing)
When daffodils begin to peer, —
With, hey! the doxy over the dale, —
Why, then comes in the sweet o' the year;
For the red blood reigns in the winter's pale.

The white sheet bleaching on the hedge, —
With, hey! the sweet birds, O, how they sing! —
Doth set my pugging tooth on edge;
For a quart of ale is a dish for a king.

The lark, that tirra-lirra chants, —
With, hey! with, hey! the thrush and the jay, —
Are summer songs for me and my aunts,
While we lie tumbling in the hay.

Autolycus: A merry heart goes all the day,
Your sad tires in a mile-a.

THE WINTER'S TALE

Act IV · Scene 3

Florizel: *Apprehend*
Nothing but jollity. The gods themselves
Humbling their deities to love, have taken
The shapes of beasts upon them: Jupiter
Became a bull, and bellow'd: the green Neptune
A ram, and bleated: and the fire-rob'd god,
Golden Apollo, a poor humble swain.

Perdita: *Daffodils,*
That come before the swallow dares, and take
The winds of March with beauty; violets dim,
But sweeter than the lids of Juno's eyes
Or Cytherea's breath, pale primroses,
That die unmarried ere they can behold
Bright Phoebus in his strength, — a malady
Most incident to maids; bold oxlips, and
The crown-imperial; lilies of all kinds,
The flower-de-luce being one! — O, these I lack,

THE WINTER'S TALE

Act IV · Scene 3

Perdita: *Sir, the year growing ancient.*
Not yet on summer's death, nor on the birth
Of trembling winter, — the fairest flowers o' the season
Are our carnations, and streak'd gillyvors,
Which some call nature's bastards: of that kind
Our rustic garden's barren: and I care not
To get slips of them.

Florizel: When you dance, I wish you
A wave o' the sea, that you might ever do
Nothing but that;

Florizel: She prizes not such trifles as these are:
The gifts she looks from me are pack'd and lock'd
Up in my heart; which I have given already,
But not deliver'd.

THE WINTER'S TALE

Act IV · Scene 3

Florizel: *And he, and more*
Than he, and men, the earth, the heaven's, and all: —
That, were I crown'd the most imperial monarch,
Thereof most worthy; were I the fairest youth
That ever made eye swerve: had force and knowledge
More than was ever man's — I would not prize them
Without her love.

Camillo: Besides, you know
Prosperity's the very bond of love,
Whose fresh complexion and whose heart together
Affliction alters.

Florizel: I am but sorry, not afeard; delay'd,
But nothing alter'd: What I was, I am:
More straining on for plucking back;

THE WINTER'S TALE

Act IV · Scene 3

Camillo: A course more promising
Than a wild dedication of yourselves
To unpath'd waters, undream'd shores, most certain
To miseries enough: no hope, help you;
But, as you shake off one, to take another:

Perdita: I was not much afeard: for once or twice
I was about to speak, and tell him plainly
The self-same sun that shines upon his court
Hides not his visage from our cottage, but
Looks on alike.

Act V · Scene 1

Cleomenes: Sir, you have done enough, and had
*   perform'd*
A saint-like sorrow: no fault could you make,
Which you have not redeem'd; indeed, paid down
More penitence than done trespass: at the last,
Do as the heavens have done, forget your evil;

Act V · Scene 3

Paulina: What, sovereign sir,
I did not well, I meant well.

King John · Act IV. Scene 1.

*Arthur: "Too fairly, Hubert, for so foul effect. Must you with
hot irons burn out both mine eyes?"*

140

KING JOHN

In 1598, an obscure man-of-letters named Francis Meres, acclaimed Shakespeare as one of the greatest writers of his time, and listed *King John* among his well-known tragedies. The work was probably written two years earlier — or, perhaps we should say, re-written; for Shakespeare borrowed much of his material from a popular play, *The Troublesome Reign of John, King of England,* produced at the beginning of the same decade, revising and recasting the text throughout, and adding pathetic and dramatic details. He also inserted Faulconbridge's famous speech:

This England never did, nor never shall,
Lie at the proud foot of a conqueror . . .

in which he gave eloquent expression to the heady chauvinism of the Elizabethan audience. More significantly, he deals with a private sorrow. Hamnet Shakespeare, the poet's only son, had died at Stratford on August 11th, 1596. The child was eleven years old; if he resembled Shakespeare, he was alert and good-looking, and, no doubt, his father's favourite. Evidently Shakespeare loved children; and he puts into Constance's mouth a lament for her son that may well have voiced his own feelings, as he remembered Hamnet so changed and wasted by sickness that he had become a phantom of his former self, or recalled how he had seen his "vacant garments" laid out across an empty bed.

KING JOHN

Act I · Scene 1

Bastard: Most certain of one mother, mighty king;
That is well known; and, as I think, one father:
But for certain knowledge of that truth,
I put you o'er to heaven and to my mother:
Of that I doubt, as all men's children may.

Lady Faulconbridge: King Richard coeur-de-lion was
       thy father;
By long and vehement suit I was seduced
To make room for him in my husband's bed —
Heaven lay not transgression to my charge!
Thou art the issue of my dear offence,
Which was so strongly urg'd, past my defence.

Act III · Scene 1

Constance: What hath this day deserv'd? what hath it
       done
That it in golden letters should be set
Among the high tides in the calendar?
Nay, rather turn this day out of the week,
This day of shame, oppression, perjury;
Or, if it must stand still, let wives with child
Pray that their burdens may not fall this day,
Lest that their hopes prodigiously be cross'd.

KING JOHN

Act III · Scene 1

Constance: War! war! no peace! peace is to me a war.
O Limoges! O Austria! thou dost shame
That bloody spoil: thou slave, thou wretch, thou
    coward!
Thou little valiant, great in villainy!
Thou ever strong upon the stronger side!
Thou fortune's champion that dost never fight
But when her humorous ladyship is by
To teach thee safety!

Act III · Scene 4

Constance: He talks to me that never had a son.
King Philip: You are as fond of grief as of your child.
Constance: Grief fills the room up of my absent child,
Lies in his bed, walks up and down with me,
Puts on his pretty looks, repeats his words,
Remembers me of all his gracious parts,
Stuffs out his vacant garments with his form;
Then have I reason to be so fond of grief.

Louis: There's nothing in this world can make me joy:
Life is as tedious as a twice-told tale
Vexing the dull ear of a drowsy man;
And bitter shame hath spoiled the sweet world's taste,
That it yields naught but shame and bitterness.
Pandulph: Before the curing of a strong disease,
Even in the instant of repair and health,
The fit is strongest; evils that take leave,
On their departure most of all show evil:
What have you lost by losing of this day?

King Richard II · Act IV. Scene 1.

King Richard: "Give me the glass . . ."

RICHARD II

The Elizabethans had a strong dramatic sense. They saw the world as a stage; and a spectacle they particularly enjoyed was afforded by the rise and fall of great men — favourites like Essex and Ralegh, who themselves often possessed a strikingly histrionic character and, when the time came for them to mount the scaffold, delivered splendid farewell speeches. The fall of an anointed sovereign provided an even more exciting subject. The idea of kingship — of the monarch as a semi-sacred being — still dominated sixteenth-century minds. To assault his person was a sacriligious gesture; which was followed, as history developed, by a train of fearful consequences. Richard II had been a weak, unworthy ruler; but nothing could excuse the conduct of Henry Bolingbroke, who had risen up against him and usurped his crown. The subject grew even more dangerous after the publication of a Papal Bull in 1596, encouraging English Catholics to dethrone Elizabeth; and the whole Abdication Scene was therefore omitted from the first Quarto Edition of *Richard II* which appeared a year later. The ill-fated king portrayed by Shakespeare is both a symbolic royal victim and one of those gifted, irresolute personages whom he afterwards summed up in the character of Hamlet. He is an artist, who collapses beneath the weight of the function that an unkind destiny has imposed on him — obstinate, arrogant, vain, yet full of sensibility and self-pity. Shakespeare's fine rhetorical drama had a curious connection with the story of the fall of Essex. In February, 1601, just before the disgraced general took up arms against the government, two of his friends approached Shakespeare's company and asked them to put on "the play of the deposing and killing of King Richard II" at the Globe Theatre next day. Evidently they felt that it would arouse popular support for the real-life drama that they were then preparing.

RICHARD II

Act I · Scene 1

Norfolk: My dear dear lord,
The purest treasure mortal times afford
Is spotless reputation; that away,
Men are but gilded loam or painted clay.

— — —

Mine honour is my life; both grow in one;
Take honour from me, and my life is done:
Then, dear my liege, mine honour let me try;
In that I live, and for that will I die.

RICHARD II

Act I · Scene 2

Duchess of Gloster: Where, then, alas,
  may I complain myself?
John of Gaunt: To God, the widow's champion
  and defence.

Duchess of Gloster: Grief boundeth where it falls,
Not with the empty hollowness, but weight:
I take my leave before I have begun;
For sorrow ends not when it seemeth done.

RICHARD II

Act I · Scene 3

King Richard: The hopeless word of never to return
Breathe I against thee, upon pain of life.
Norfolk: A heavy sentence, my most sovereign liege,
And all unlook'd-for from your highness' mouth,
A dearer merit, not so deep a maim
As to be cast forth in the common air,
Have I deserved at your highness' hands.
The language I have learn'd these forty years,
My native English, now I must forgo:

John of Gaunt: All places that the eye of heaven visits
Are to a wise man ports and happy havens.
Teach thy necessity to reason thus;
There is no virtue like necessity.

Bolingbroke: Then England's ground, farewell, sweet
*   soil, adieu;*
My mother, and my nurse, that bears me yet!
Where'er I wander boast of this I can, —
Though banish'd yet a true-born Englishman.

RICHARD II

Act II · Scene 1

John of Gaunt: This fortress built by Nature for herself
Against infection and the hand of war;
This happy breed of men, this little world;
This precious stone set in the silver sea,
Which serves it in the office of a wall,
Or as a moat defensive to a house,
Against the envy of less happier lands;
This blessed plot, this earth, this realm, this England,

King Richard: For God's sake, let us sit upon the
      ground,
And tell sad stories of the death of kings: —
How some have been depos'd; some slain in war;
Some haunted by the ghosts they have depos'd;
Some poison'd by their wives; some sleeping kill'd;
All murder'd: — for within the hollow crown
That rounds the mortal temples of a king
Keeps Death his court; and there the antic sits,
Scoffing his state, and grinning at his pomp;
Allowing him a breath, a little scene,
To monarchize, be fear'd, and kill with looks;
Infusing him with self and vain conceit, —
As if this flesh, which walls about our life,
Were brass impregnable; and humour'd thus,
Comes at the last, and with a little pin
Bores through his castle-wall, and — farewell, king!

RICHARD II

Act III · Scene 3

Queen: And am I last that knows it? O thou think'st
To serve me last, that I may longest keep
Thy sorrow in my breast. — Come ladies, go,
To meet in London, London's king in woe —

Act IV · Scene 1

King Richard: Here cousin, seize the crown;
On this side my hand, and on that side yours.
Now is this golden crown like a deep well
That owes two buckets, filling one another;
The emptier ever dancing in the air,
The other down, unseen, and full of water:
That bucket down and full of tears am I,
Drinking my griefs, whilst you mount up on high.

RICHARD II

Act V · Scene 1

King Richard: Doubly divorc'd! — Bad men, you violate
A twofold marriage — 'twixt my crown and me,
And then betwixt me and my married wife. —
Let me unkiss the oath 'twixt thee and me;
And yet not so, for with a kiss 'twas made. —
Part us, Northumberland; I towards the north,
Where shivering cold and sickness pines the clime,
My wife to France — from whence; set forth in pomp
She came adorned hither like sweet May,
Sent back like Hallowmas or short'st of day.

Act V · Scene 5

King Richard: How sour sweet music is
When time is broke and no proportion kept!
So is it the music of men's lives,
And here have I the daintiness of ear
To check time broke in a disorder'd string;
But, for the concord of my state and time,
Had not an ear to hear my true time broke.

King Henry IV Part one · Act II. Scene 4.

Poins: "Welcome, Jack: where hast thou been?"

152

HENRY IV

Of all Shakespeare's great historical dramas, the most impressive, most various, and most densely "rammed with life" is his two-fold play on the reign of King Henry IV. Its chief character is a guilty man; he has violated the sacred laws of kingship; and every trouble that overtakes him is derived ultimately from that supreme offence. His plight is symbolic; but Shakespeare, we feel, was far less interested in symbols than in individual human beings; and, while Henry himself is drawn with skill and sympathy, Hotspur, Glendower and Falstaff are creations of high poetic genius. Falstaff, indeed, though introduced to provide comic relief, becomes a hero in his own right, and, as Mercutio had done in *Romeo and Juliet*, soon threatens to dominate the whole stage. This is the more remarkable since Shakespeare had borrowed Falstaff from an old play, entitled *The Famous Victories of Henry V*, written about 1586. None of Shakespeare's other characters has commanded so much personal affection. Among the "iron men" who surround him, and who think in terms of past and future, Falstaff is the *homme moyen sensuel*, whose concern is with the pleasures of the present day. Even that stern moralist Samuel Johnson paid him an unexpected tribute: "Falstaff, unimitated, inimitable Falstaff, how shall I describe thee! Thou compound of sense and vice; of sense which may be admired . . . of vice which may be despised, but hardly detested". There is no doubt that "the fat knight" contributed enormously to the play's success, when it was first produced in 1597 or 1598.

HENRY IV

Act I · Scene 2

Falstaff: Now, Hal, what time of day is it lad?
Prince Henry: Thou art so fat-witted with drinking of
old sack, and unbuttoning thee after supper, and
sleeping upon benches after noon, that thou hast
forgotten to demand that truly which thou would'st
truly know. What a devil hast thou to do with the time
of the day?

Prince Henry: Thou didst well; for wisdom cries out
in the streets, and no man regards it.
Falstaff: O, thou hast damnable iteration, and art,
indeed, able to corrupt a saint. Thou hast done much
harm upon me, Hal, — God forgive thee for it! Before
I knew thee, Hal, I knew nothing; and now am I, if a
man should speak truly, little better than one of the
wicked.

Prince Henry: If all the year were playing holidays,
To sport would be as tedious as to work ;
But when they seldom come, they wish'd-for come,
And nothing pleaseth but rare accidents.

Act II · Scene 3

Lady Percy: O my good lord, why are you thus alone?
For what offence have I this fortnight been
A banish'd woman from my Harry's bed?
Tell me sweet lord, what is't that takes from thee
Thy stomach, pleasure, and thy golden sleep?

HENRY IV

Act II · Scene 4

*Falstaff: You rogue, here's lime in this sack too;
there is nothing but roguery to be found in villanous
man: yet a coward is worse than a cup of sack with
lime in it, — a villanous coward. — Go thy ways old
Jack; die when thou wilt, if manhood, good manhood,
be not forgot upon the face of the earth, then am I a
shotten herring.*

*Falstaff: Harry, I do not only marvel where thou
spendest thy time, but also how thou art accompanied:
for though the camomile, the more it is trodden on,
the faster it grows, yet youth, the more it is wasted
the sooner it wears.*

Act V · Scene 2

*Hotspur: O gentlemen, the time of life is very short!
To spend that shortness basely were too long,
If life did ride upon a dial's point,
Still ending at the arrival of an hour.*

Act V · Scene 4

*Percy Hotspur: But thought's the slave of life,
        and life time's fool;
And time, that takes survey of all the world,
Must have a stop.*

HENRY IV Part two

Act I · Scene 1

Earl of Northumberland: The times are wild;
* contention, like a horse,*
Full of high feeding, madly hath broke loose
And bears down all before him.

Act I · Scene 2

Falstaff: Virtue is of so little regard in these
costermonger times that true valour is turn'd
bear-herd: pregnancy is made a tapster, and hath his
quick wit wasted in giving reckonings: all the other
gifts appertinent to man, as the malice of this age
shapes them; are not worth a gooseberry.

Falstaff: The truth is, I am only old in judgment and
understanding; and he that will caper with me for a
thousand marks, let him lend me the money, and have
at him. For the box o' the ear that the prince gave
you, — he gave it like a rude prince, and you took it
like a sensible lord. I have check'd him for it; and the
young lion repents, — marry, not in ashes and sack-
cloth, but in new silk and old sack.

Falstaff: If I do, fillip me with a three-man beetle —
A man can no more separate age and covetousness
than a can part young limbs and lechery: but the gout
galls the one, and the pox pinches the other.

HENRY IV Part two

Act III · Scene 1

King Henry: How many thousand of my poorest subjects
Are at this hour asleep! — O sleep, O gentle sleep,
Nature's soft nurse, how have I frighted thee,
That thou no more wilt weigh my eyelids down,
And steep my senses in forgetfulness?

King Henry: Then, happy low, lie down!
Uneasy lies the head that wears a crown.

Earl of Warwick: There is a history
*   in all men's lives,*
Figuring the nature of the times deceas'd;
The which observ'd, a man may prophesy,
With a near aim, of the main chance of things
As yet come to life, which in their seeds
And weak beginnings lie intreasured.

Act III · Scene 2

Shallow: Ha, cousin Silence, that thou hadst
seen that that this knight and I have seen! — Ha,
Sir John, said I well?

Falstaff: We have heard the chimes at midnight,
Master Shallow.

HENRY IV Part two

Act IV · Scene 3

Falstaff: A good sherris-sack hath a twofold operation in it. It ascends me into the brain; dries me there all the foolish and dull and crudy vapours which environ it; makes it apprenensive, quick, forgetive, full of nimble, fiery, and delectable shapes; which delivered o'er to the voice, — the tongue, — which is the birth, becomes excellent wit. The second property of your excellent sherris is, — the warming of the blood;

Falstaff: Hereof comes it that Prince Harry is valiant: for the cold blood he did naturally inherit of his father, he hath, like lean, sterile, and bare land, manured, husbanded, and tilled, with excellent endeavour of drinking good and good store of fertile sherris, that he is become very hot and valiant.

Act IV · Scene 4

King Henry: Most subject is the fattest soil to weeds;

Ear of Warwick: My gracious lord,
*   you look beyond him quite:*
The prince but studies his companions
Like a strange tongue; wherein, to gain the language,
'Tis needful that the most immodest word
Be look'd upon and learn'd; which once attain'd,
Your highness knows, comes to no further use
But to be known and hated.

HENRY IV Part two

Act IV · Scene 4

Prince Henry: No; I will sit and watch here by the king.
Why doth the crown lie there upon his pillow,
Being so troublesome a bedfellow?
O polish'd perturbation! golden care!
That keep'st the ports of slumber open wide
To many watchful night! — sleep with it now!
Yet not so sound and half so deeply sweet
As he whose brow with homely biggen bound
Snores out the watch of night.

Prince John: Health, peace, and happiness to my royal
       father!
King Henry: Thou bring'st me happiness and peace,
       son John;
But health, alack, with youthful wings is flown
From this bare wither'd trunk: upon the sight
My worldly business makes a period.

Act V · Scene 3

Silence [singing]: Be merry, be merry, my wife has all
For women are shrews, both short and tall:
'Tis merry in hall when beards wag all,
And welcome merry Shrovetide.
Be merry, be merry.

King Henry V · Act IV. Scene 1.

Pistol: "Discuss unto me ; art thou officer?"

HENRY V

Despite the strong appeal that it has always made to patriotic English audiences, *Henry V* is a far less interesting work than *Henry II* or even *Richard III*. Price Hal re-emerges as King Henry; the lively, dissipated young man becomes a stern self-righteous martinet. He dismisses and humiliates his old friend Falstaff; and Falstaff, as Hazlitt remarks, was undeniably "the better man of the two. We think of him and quote him oftener". Shakespeare celebrates King Henry's soldierly virtues and makes a generous allowance for his martial vices. He accepts the fact that Henry was a man of blood, and gives him a repellent speech in which he threatens the citizens of Harfleur, not only with beholding the destruction of their city, but with seeing their children massacred and their virgin daughters ravished. But then, Shakespeare addressed the patriots of his day; and Elizabethan methods of warfare were still as barbarous as those of the Middle Ages. Essex headed the English war-party; and, in his prologue to the fifth act, Shakespeare pictures the General returning from Ireland "bringing rebellion broached on his sword . . ." *Henry V* must, therefore, have been written and staged between March and October, 1599. Although the play contains some splendid passages of verse, it seldom rises to the highest level, either dramatic or poetic; and Shakespeare's genius is confined to the scene where the Hostess, Pistol, Nym and Bardolph rehearse the story of Falstaff's recent death. Of Henry himself, it has been said by John Masefield that he is "one commonplace man" in Shakespeare's English historical dramas.

HENRY V

Act I · Scene 1

Archbishop of Canterbury: The courses of his youth
*   promis'd it not.*
The breath no sooner left his father's body,
But that his wildness, mortified in him,
Seem'd to die too: yea, at that very moment,
Consideration, like an angel, came,
And whipp'd th' offending Adam out of him,
Leaving his body as a paradise,
To envelop and contain celestial spirits.
Never was such a sudden scholar made.

Act II · Scene 3

Pistol: Falstaff he is dead,
And we must yearn therefore.
Bardolph: Would I were with him, wheresome'er
he is, either in heaven or in hell!
Hostess: Nay, sure he's not in hell: he's in Arthur's
bosom, if ever man went to Arthur's bosom. 'A made a
finer end, and went away, an it had been any
christom child; 'a parted even just between twelve and
one, even at the turning o' the tide: for after I saw
him fumble with the sheets, and play with flowers, and
smile upon his fingers' ends, I knew there was but one
way; for his nose was as sharp as a pen, and 'a
babbled of green fields. . . . .

So 'a bade me lay more clothes on his feet: I put my
hand into the bed and felt them, and they were as cold
as any stone; then I felt to his knees, and so upward
and upward, and all was as cold as any stone.

HENRY V

Act II · Scene 4

Dauphin: In cases of defence 'tis best to weigh
The enemy more mighty than he seems:

Act III · Scene 1

King Henry: In peace there's nothing so becomes a man
As modest stillness and humility:
But when the blast of war blows in our ears,
Then imitate the action of the tiger;

Act IV · Prologue

Chorus: The hum of either army stilly sounds,
That the fix'd sentinels almost receive
The secret whispers of each other's watch:
Fire answers fire, and through their paly flames
Each battle sees the other's umber'd face:
Steed threatens steed, in high and boastful neighs
Piercing the night's dull ear; and from the tents
The armourers, accomplishing the knights,
With busy hammers closing rivets up,
Give dreadful note of preparation:
The country cocks do crow, the clocks do toll,
And the third hour of drowsy morning name.

HENRY VI

The young Shakespeare probably reached London in 1587 or 1588. The latter was a momentous year, heralded by many omens; for, that summer, the gigantic Spanish fleet, the Invincible Armada, launched by Philip II against the English realm, was triumphantly repulsed and scattered; and, during the same year, the Queen's favourite the great Earl of Leicester, whom it was once expected she would marry, died at the age of fifty-six. The defeat of the Spanish Armada filled Englishmen with a passionate interest in their own history; thenceforward a patriotic drama would always draw a London audience; and among those who exploited the current demand was the apprentice-playwright William Shakespeare. His first efforts were the three parts of *Henry VI*, which some believe that he wrote unaided, others in collaboration with a team of fellow hacks. It is a chronicle-play, a serialization of historical events, rather than an adult drama, covering the end of the long-drawn French War and the genesis of the internecine Wars of the Roses; and, in Part III, the future Richard III emerges as one of Shakespeare's most tremendous villains. The play scored an immediate popular success; but it was the Talbot episode that drew the loudest plaudits. "How would it have joyed brave Talbot . . .", wrote Thomas Nashe in 1592, "to think that, after he had lain two hundred years in his tomb, he should triumph again on the stage, and have his bones new-embalmed with the tears of ten thousand spectators at least . . ." Shakespeare was now generally recognised as a rising modern dramatist.

HENRY VI Part one

Act I · Scene I

Bedford: Henry the fifth too famous to live long!
England ne'er lost a king of so much worth.
Gloster: England ne'er had a king until his time.
Virtue he had, deserving to command;
His brandish'd sword did blind men with his beams;
His arms spread wider than a dragon's wings.

Act I · Scene 5

La Pucelle: Advance our waving colours on the walls;
Rescu'd is Orleans from the English: —
Thus Joan la Pucelle hath perform'd her word.
Charles: Divinest creature, Astræa's daughter,
How shall I honour thee for this success?
Thy promises are like Adonis' gardens,
That one day bloom'd and fruitful were the next.

Act III · Scene 3

La Pucelle: Care is no cure, but rather corrosive,
For things that are not to be remedied.

Act V · Scene 5

Suffolk: For what is wedlock forced but a hell,
An age of discord and continual strife?
Whereas the contrary bringeth bliss,
And is a pattern of celestial peace.

King Henry VI First part   Act I. Scene 5.

Talbot pursuing the Dauphin.

166

HENRY VI Part two

Act I · Scene 1

King Henry: *Welcome, Queen Margaret;*
I can express no kinder sign of love
Than this kind kiss. — O Lord, that lends me life,
Lend me a heart replete with thankfulness!
For thou hast given me, in this beauteous face,
A world of earthly blessings to my soul,
If sympathy of love unite our thoughts.

Earl of Salisbury: Pride went before,
    ambition follows him.

Act II · Scene 4

Duke of Gloster: Thus sometimes hath the brightest day a cloud;
And after summer evermore succeeds
Barren winter, with his wrathful nipping cold;
So cares and joys abound, as seasons fleet.

Act III · Scene 1

Queen Margaret: Now 'tis the spring, and weeds are
shallow-rooted; Suffer them now, and they'll o'ergrow the
garden, And choke the herbs for want of husbandry.

Suffolk: Smooth runs the water where the brook is deep:
And in his simple show he harbours treason.
The fox barks not when he would steal the lamb.

HENRY VI Part two

Act III · Scene 2

Queen Margaret: Mischance and sorrow go along
*   with you!*
Heart's discontent and sour affliction
Be playfellows to keep you company!
There's two of you; the devil make the third!
And threefold vengeance tend upon your steps!

Act IV · Scene 6

Dick: My lord there's an army gather'd together
*   in Smithfield.*
Jack Cade: Come, then, let's go fight with them;
but first, — go and set London-bridge on fire, and, if
you can, burn down the Tower too. Come, let's away.

Act V · Scene 1

Salisbury: It is great sin to swear unto a sin;
But greater sin to keep a sinful oath.
Who can be bound by any solemn vow
To do a murderous deed, to rob a man,
To force a spotless virgin's chastity,
To reave the orphan of his patrimony,
To wring the widow from her custom'd right;
And have no other reason for this wrong,
But that he was bound by a solemn oath?

HENRY VI Part three

Act II · Scene 5

*King Henry: Would I were dead! if God's good
     will were so;
For what is in this world but grief and woe?
O God! methinks it were a happy life
To be no better than a homely swain;
To sit upon a hill, as I do now,
To carve out dials quaintly point by point,
Thereby to see the minutes, how they run.
How many makes the hour full complete.*

Act IV · Scene 3

*King Edward: What fates impose,
     that men must needs abide;
It boots not to resist both wind and tide.*

Act V · Scene 4

*Queen Margaret: Great lords, wise men ne'er sit
     and wail their loss,
But cheerly seek how to redress their harms.
What though the mast be now blown overboard,
The cable broke, the holding-anchor lost,
And half our sailors swallow'd in the flood;
Yet lives our pilot still:*

King Richard III · Act I. Scene 1.

Richard, Duke of Gloster: "I am determined to prove a villain . . ."

RICHARD III

From one point of view. Richard of Gloucester is the stock
Elizabethan desperado, who announces that he means "to
prove a villain" at the first convenient opportunity. But,
although *Richard III* is an early play, written before 1594,
Shakespeare also portrays him as an imaginative and introspective character. He hates mankind because he hates
himself; but, underlying his self-hatred, there runs a strain of
fierce self-love. Like other Shakespearian tragic personages,
he is isolated by his own unruly passions; he cannot escape
from the confinement of the self and rages furiously against
his solitude. Richard seems to have been Shakespeare's
earliest attempt to depict the real complexity of human nature,
to show how evil takes root in a human soul, and how absolute
power may corrupt a fine intelligence. As an historian, however, Shakespeare shared the limitations of his age. Although
modern writers have sometimes credited him with what one
of them calls "a steady political earnestness" and an experienced grasp of statecraft, his vision of English victory was
comparatively simple. His object was to glorify King Henry
VII, grand-father of Queen Elizabeth, by blackening the
tyrant he had overcome and slain, and to draw a comparison
between the benefits of Tudor rule and the bloody chaos of
the previous period. Richard III is a part that has always
fascinated English actors. In Shakespeare's day it was played,
with immense success, by the renowned tragedian 'Edward
Alleyn.

RICHARD III

Act I · Scene 1

Gloster: Now is the winter of our discontent
Made glorious summer by this sun of York;
And all the clouds that lower'd upon our house
In the deep bosom of the ocean buried.
Now are our brows bound with victorious wreaths;
Our bruised arms hung up for monuments;
Our stern alarums chang'd to merry meetings,
Our dreadful marches to delightful measures.
Grim-visag'd war hath smooth'd his wrinkled front;
And now, — instead of mounting barbed steeds
To fright the souls of fearful adversaries, —
He capers nimbly in a lady's chamber
To the lascivious pleasing of a lute.
But I, that am not shap'd for sportive tricks,
Nor made to court an amorous looking-glass;
I, that am rudely stamp'd, and want love's majesty
To strut before a wanton ambling nymph;
I, that am curtail'd of this fair proportion,
Cheated of feature by dissembling nature,
Deform'd, unfinish'd, sent before my time
Into this breathing world scarce half made up,
And that so lamely and unfashionable
That dogs bark at me as I halt by them; —
Why, I, in this weak piping time of peace,
Have no delight to pass away the time,
Unless to spy my shadow in the sun,
And descant on mine own deformity:
And therefore, — since I cannot prove a lover,
To entertain these fair well-spoken days, —
I am determined to prove a villain,
And hate the idle pleasures of these days.

RICHARD III

Act III · Scene 1

*Prince Edward: Methinks the truth should live
    from age to age,
As 'twere retail'd to all posterity,
Even to the general all-ending day.
Gloster (aside): So wise so young, they say,
    do never live long.*

Act V · Scene 3

*King Richard: What, do I fear myself?
    there's none else by:
Richard loves Richard; that is, I am I.
Is there a murderer here? No; — yes; I am:
Then fly. What, from myself? Great reason why, —
Lest I revenge. What, — myself upon myself!
Alack, I love myself. Wherefore? for any good
That I myself have done unto myself?
O, no! alas, I rather hate myself
For hateful deeds committed by myself!
I am a villain: yet I lie, I am not.*

*King Richard: A horse! a horse! my kingdom for a
    horse!
Catesley: Withdraw, my lord; I'll help you to a horse!*

King Henry VIII · Act III. Scene 2.

Cardinal Wolsey: "Farewell, a long farewell, to all my greatness!"

HENRY VIII

With *Henry VIII*, which was among his last plays*— those written after 1608 — Shakespeare brought to an end his great sequence of English historical dramas. The action culminates in the christening of the future Queen Elizabeth; and, having shown how the triumphant Tudor dynasty had restored the rule of law and order, he makes Cranmer prophesy the advent of a sovereign who will illustrate all the virtues of her line. As a work of art, the play is extremely uneven; and it is thought that, although the first three acts were composed by Shakespeare, a collaborator — possibly John Fletcher — may have been responsible for the concluding scenes. Wolsey's magnificent valediction has the true Shakespearian ring:

Farewell! a long farewell, to all my greatness!
This is the state of man: today he puts forth
The tender leaves of hope; tomorrow blossoms . . .
The third day comes a frost, a killing frost . . .

But later episodes seem merely to provide an excuse for the kind of pageants and masquerades that a Jacobean audience favoured. Whenever the play was begun, it was presented as "a new play" on June 29th, 1613. On that occasion, a piece of stage artillery set fire to the thatched roof of the venerable Globe Theatre; and the "virtuous fabric", that had seen so many of Shakespeare's successes, went up in flames and was completely gutted.

HENRY VIII

Act I · Scene 1

Norfolk: Stay, my lord,
And let your reason with your choler question
What 'tis you go about: To climb steep hills
Requires slow pace at first: anger is like
A full-hot horse, who being allow'd his way,
Self-mettle tires him. Not a man in England
Can advise me like you: be to yourself
As you would to your friend.

Norfolk: Be advis'd:
Heat not a furnace for your foe so hot
That it do singe yourself: we may outrun,
By violent swiftness, that which we run at,
And lose by over-running.

Act II · Scene 2

Lord Chamberlain: It seems the marriage with his
brother's wife
Has crept too near his conscience.
Suffolk: No, his conscience
Has crept too near another lady.

Act II · Scene 3

Old lady: If your back
Cannot vouchsafe this burden, 'tis too weak
Ever to get a boy.
Anne Bullen: How you do talk!
I swear again, I would not be a queen
For all the world.

HENRY VIII

Act III · Scene 1

Queen Katharine: Have I liv'd thus long — let me
    speak myself,
Since virtue finds no friends, — a wife a true one?
A woman, — I dare say without vain glory, —
Never yet branded with suspicion?
Have I with all my full affections
Still met the king? lov'd him next heaven?
    obey'd him?
Been, out of fondness, superstitious to him?
Almost forgot my prayers to content him?
And I am thus rewarded?

Act III · Scene 2

Wolsey: Farewell, a long farewell, to all my greatness!
This is the state of man: today he puts forth
The tender leaves of hope; to-morrow blossoms,
And bears his blushing honours thick upon him;
The third day comes a frost, a killing frost,
And, — when he thinks, good easy man, full surely
His greatness is a-ripening, — nips his root,
And then he falls, as I do

Wolsey: Go, get thee from me Cromwell;
I am a poor fallen man, unworthy now
To be thy lord and master: seek the king;
That sun I pray, may never set! I have told him
What and how true thou art.

Coriolanus · Act II. Scene 1.

Coriolanus: "My gracious silence, hail!"

CORIOLANUS

Compared with many other Shakespearean tragedies, *Corio-lanus* is a monolithic play. It seems to have been hewn out of a single block; the effect is massive, splendid, uniform. Pride is the theme — the pride of a man who, like Essex, cannot "carry his honours even". Shakespeare's source-book was North's translation of Plutarch; and he follows the historian's portrait closely. "He was a man", wrote Plutarch, "too full of passion and choler . . . that remembered not how wilfulness is a thing . . . which a governor of a commonwealth . . . should shun, being that which Plato called 'solitariness'" . . . Shakespeare's Coriolanus is, above all else, a solitary man; cut off by his over-weening pride, he remains "a lonely dragon", and, because he cannot communicate, brings ruin upon himself and near-disaster upon his fellow citizens. Yet Coriolanus is not entirely devoid of feeling; he reveres his mother, and loves and respects his wife. Nor is he incapable of arousing love. Just as Falstaff loves Prince Henry, so the Falstaffian senator Menenius loves the young man who has become his "son"; and the scene in which the General rejects Menenius is a particularly moving episode. Despite its monumental character, the play is full of pathetic human touches; and these touches are doubly effective against their severe and sombre background. We do not know where *Coriolanus* was first performed, whether at Court or at the Globe Theatre; but it was written about 1607 or 1608, and closes the sequence of tragedies that had begun with *Hamlet*.

CORIOLANUS

Act I · Scene 3

*Volumnia: I pray your daughter, sing or express
yourself in a more comfortable sort: if my son were
my husband, I should freelier rejoice in that absence
wherein he won honour than in the embracements of
his bed where he would show most love.*

Act I · Scene 6

*Cominius: Breathe you, my friends: well fought;
     we are come off
Like Romans, neither foolish in our stands
Nor cowardly in retire: believe me, sirs,
We shall be charg'd again.*

Act II · Scene 1

*Menenius: I am known to be a humorous patrician,
and one that loves a cup of hot wine with not a drop of
allaying Tiber in 't: said to be something imperfect in
favouring the first complaint, hasty and tinder-like
upon too trivial motion; one that converses more with
the buttock of the night than with the forehead of the
morning.*

CORIOLANUS

Act V · Scene 3

Coriolanus: Like a dull actor now,
I have forgot my part, and I am out,
Even to a full disgrace. Best of my flesh,
Forgive my tyranny; but do not say,
For that, "Forgive our Romans". — O, a kiss
Long as my exile, sweet as my revenge;
Now, by the jealous queen of heaven, that kiss
I carried from thee, dear; and my true lip
Hath virgin'd it e'er since. — You gods! I prate,
And the most noble mother of the world
Leave unsaluted:

Coriolanus: O mother, mother!
What have you done? Behold, the heaven do ope,
The gods look down, and this unnatural scene
They laugh at. O my mother, mother! O!
You have won a happy victory to Rome;
But for your son, — believe it, O, believe it,
Most dangerously you have with him prevail'd,

Volumnia: He turns away:
Down, ladies; let us shame him with our knees.
To his surname Coriolanus 'longs more pride
Than pity to our prayers. Down: an end;
This is the last. — So we will home to Rome,
And die among our neighbours.

Titus Andronicus · Act V. Scene 3.

Titus kills Tamora.

TITUS ANDRONICUS

In 1587 two horrific tragedies revolutionised the English drama — Christopher Marlowe's *Tamburlaine the Great* and Thomas Kyd's *The Spanish Tragedy*. The latter was a particularly successful play and attracted audiences for another five decades; it was often imitated and parodied by later Elizabethan dramatists. Among its early imitators was William Shakespeare, whose *Titus Andronicus*, a work in the same style, appeared at the beginning of the fifteen-nineties. Like Kyd's masterpiece, it involved revenge and bloodshed; but Shakespeare piled horror on horror with even greater assiduity and skill, adding some touches of poetic brilliance. Oddly enough, this crude and violent production retained its popularity throughout his lifetime; and Ben Jonson complained in 1614 that "he that will swear that Ieronimo [*The Spanish Tragedy*] or Andronicus are the best plays yet shall pass unexcepted ... as a man whose judgment shows it is constant, and hath stood still these five-and-twenty or thirty years . . ." But *Titus Andronicus* has another distinction. It was long supposed that Shakespeare's characters assumed the apparel of his own age; that Mark Antony may have worn a doublet and trunk-hose, and Cleopatra an Elizabethan farthingale. Recently, however, there has come to light a manuscript copy of *Titus Andronicus*, made in 1595, with a rough illustration of the scene between Tamora and the Emperor. Here the chief actors are arrayed in classical dress, as pictured by a sixteenth-century artist; while only their attendant guards are equipped with modern clothes and weapons.

TITUS ANDRONICUS

Act I · Scene 1

Tamora, queen of the Goths: Wilt thou draw near the
nature of the gods?
Draw near them, then, in being merciful:
Sweet mercy is nobility's true badge:

Titus: Here lurks no treason, here no envy swells,
Here grows no damned grudges; here are no storms,
No noise, but silence and eternal sleep:

Act II · Scene 1

Demetrius: She is a woman, therefore may be woo'd;
She is a woman, therefore may be won;
She is Lavinia, therefore must be lov'd.
What, man! more water glideth by the mill
Than wots the miller of; and easy it is
Of a cut loaf to steal a shive, we know.

Act II · Scene 2

Titus: The hunt is up, the morn is bright and gay,
The fields are fragrant, and the woods are green.
Uncouple here, and let us make a bay.

TITUS ANDRONICUS

Act II · Scene 3

Tamora: The birds chant melody on every bush;
The snake lies rolled in the cheerful sun;
The green leaves quiver with the cooling wind,
And make a chequer'd shadow on the ground:

Act II · Scene 4

Marcus Andronicus: Sorrow concealed, like an
*   oven stopp'd,*
Doth burn the heart to cinders where it is.

Act III · Scene 2

Titus Andronicus: But how, if that fly had a father
*   and a mother?*
How would he hang his slender gilded wings,
And buzz lamenting doings in the air!
Poor harmless fly,
That with his pretty buzzing melody
Came here to make us merry!
And thou hast kill'd him.

Act V · Scene 1

Aaron: Yet for I know thou art religious,
And hast a thing within thee called conscience,
With twenty papish tricks and ceremonies,
Which I have seen thee careful to observe,
Therefore I urge thy oath.

Romeo and Juliet · Act 11. Scene 2.

Romeo: "But, soft! what light through yonder window breaks?

186

ROMEO AND JULIET

Shakespeare's best-loved romantic play belongs to the second period of his literary evolution — from 1594 to 1600 — when he had mastered his craft and was rapidly perfecting his art, but still on occasions wrote clumsily and awkwardly, as in the interminable "message speech" delivered by the good Friar Lawrence. Here his source-book was a versified English rendering of a popular Italian novel. Shakespeare, of course, had never visited Italy; and his dramatis personae recall the inhabitants of Elizabethan London rather than the citizens of Verona. Mercutio seems to be a portrait of some talkative young London gentleman; the retainers of the Montagues and Capulets, "biting their thumbs" at one another and exchanging insults, recall the behaviour of the "long-sworded" braggarts who, in Shakespeare's life-time, thronged St. Paul's Church. Juliet's Nurse, too — one of the playwright's finest creations — is an extraordinarily English character. The play is full of bawdy jokes, a type of humour that the Elizabethans relished. It also displays Shakespeare's poetic genius at its most lyrical and most exalted. "The dominating image", writes Professor Spurgeon in her book on *Shakespeare's Imagery*, "is *light*, every form and manifestation of it" — the torches and tapers that illuminate the Capulets' ball; the moonlight that floods their sleeping garden; the "envious streaks" of dawn that part the lovers. Juliet appears at a brightly lit window; and she compares the effect of Romeo's declaration to a sheet of summer lightning, which glimmers suddenly across the heavens. For the theme of Shakespeare's play is not only the beauty and strength of young love but its tragic evanescence.

ROMEO AND JULIET

Prologue

Chorus: Two households, both alike in dignity,
In fair Verona, where we lay our scene,
From ancient grudge break to new mutiny,
Where civil blood makes civil hands unclean.

Act I · Scene 2

Capulet: But saying o'er what I have said before:
My child is yet a stranger to the world,
She hath not seen the change of fourteen years;
Let two more summers wither in their pride
Ere we may think her ripe to be a bride.

Capulet: Such comforts as do lusty young men feel
When well-apparell'd April on the heel
Of limping winter treads, even such delight
Among fresh female buds shall you this night
Inherit at my house;

Benvolio: One pain is lessen'd by another's anguish;
Turn giddy, and be holp by backward turning;
One desperate grief cures with another's languish:
Take thou some new infection to thy eye.
And the rank poison of the old will die.

ROMEO AND JULIET

Act I · Scene 3

Nurse: Even or odd, of all days in the year,
Come Lammas-eve at night shall she be fourteen.
Susan and she, — God rest all Christian souls! —
Were of an age: well, Susan is with God;
She was too good for me: — but, as I said,
On Lammas-eve at night shall she be fourteen;
That shall she, marry; I remember it well.
'Tis since the earthquake now eleven years;
And she was wean'd, — I never shall forget it, —
Of all the days of the year, upon that day:
For I had then laid wormwood to my dug,
Sitting in the sun under the dove-house wall;
My lord and you were than at Mantua:
Nay, I do bear a brain: — but, as, I said
When it did taste the wormwood on the nipple
Of my dug, and felt it bitter, pretty fool,.
To see it tetchy, and fall out with the dug!
Shake, quoth the dove-house: 'twas no need, I trow,
To bid me trudge.
And since that time it is eleven years;
For then she could stand alone; nay, by the rood
She could have run and waddled all about;
For even the day before, she broke her brow:
And then my husband, — God be with his soul;
'A was a merry man, — took up the child:
Yea, quoth he, dost thou fall upon they face?
Thou wilt fall backward when thou hast more wit;
Wilt thou not, Jule? and, by my holidame,
The pretty wretch left crying, and said Ay:
To see, now, how a just shall come about!
I warrant, an I should live a thousand years,
I never should forget it: Wilt thou not, Jule? quoth he;
And, pretty fool, it stinted, and said Ay.

ROMEO AND JULIET

Act I · Scene 4

Romeo: Is love a tender thing? it is too rough,
Too rude, too boisterous; and it pricks like thorn.

Mercutio: This is that very Mab
That plats the manes of horses in the night;
And bakes the elf-locks in foul sluttish hairs,
Which, once untangled, much misfortunes bodes:
This is the hag, when maids lie on their backs,
That presses them, and learns them first to bear,
Making them women of good carriage:

Act I · Scene 5

Juliet: Go, ask his name — if he be married,
My grave is like to be my wedding-bed.
Nurse: His name is Romeo, and a Montague,
The only son of your great enemy.
Juliet: My only love sprung from my only hate!
Too early seen unknown and known to late!

Romeo: She speaks: —
O, speak again, bright angel! for thou art
As glorious to this night, being o'er my head,
As is a winged messenger of heaven
Unto the white-upturned wondering eyes
Of mortals that fall back to gaze on him
When he bestrides the lazy-pacing clouds
And sails upon the bosom of the air.

ROMEO AND JULIET

Act II · Scene 2

Juliet: O, Romeo, Romeo! wherefore art thou
Romeo?
Deny thy father and refuse thy name;
Or, if thou will not, be but sworn my love,
And I'll no longer be a Capulet.

Juliet: What's in a name? that which we call a rose,
By any other name would smell as sweet;
So Romeo would, were he not Romeo call'd,
Retain that dear perfection which he owes
Without that title:

Romeo: I take thee at thy word:
Call me but love, and I'll be new baptiz'd;
Henceforth I never will be Romeo.

Romeo: With love's light wings
did I o'erperch these walls;
For stony limits cannot hold love out:
And what love can do, that dares love attempt;
Therefore thy kinsmen are no let to me.

Juliet: This bud of love, by summer's ripening breath,
May prove a beauteous flower when next we meet.
Good night, good night! as sweet repose and rest
Come to thy heart as that within my breast!

ROMEO AND JULIET

Act II · Scene 2

Juliet: My bounty is as boundless as the sea,
My love as deep; the more I give to thee
The more I have, for both are infinite.

Romeo: O blessed, blessed night! I am afeard,
Being in night, all this is but a dream,
Too flattering — sweet to be substantial.

Romeo: It is my soul that calls upon my name:
How silver-sweet sound lovers' tongues by night,
Like softest music to attending ears!

Romeo: I would I were thy bird.
Juliet: Sweet, so would I:
Yet I should kill thee with much cherishing.
Good night, good night! parting is such sweet sorrow,
That I shall say good night till it be morrow.

Act II · Scene 3

Friar Lawrence: Care keeps his wrath in every
        old man's eye,
And where care lodges sleep will never lie;
But where unbruised youth with unstuff'd brain
Doth couch his limbs, there golden sleep doth reign:

ROMEO AND JULIET

Act II · Scene 3

Friar Lawrence: I must up-fill this osier cage of ours
With baleful weeds and precious-juiced flowers.
The earth, that's nature's mother, is her tomb,
What is her burying grave, that is her womb:

Friar Lawrence: Holy Saint Francis, what a
*   change is here!*
Is Rosaline, whom thou didst love so dear,
So soon forsaken? young men's love, then, lies
Not truly in their hearts, but in their eyes.

Act II · Scene 5

Juliet: Love's heralds should be thoughts,
Which ten times faster glide than the sun's beams,
Driving back shadows over lowering hills:

Act II · Scene 6

Friar Lawrence: Here comes the lady: —
*   O, so light a foot*
Will ne'er wear out the everlasting flint:
A lover may bestride the gossamer
That idles in the wanton summer air
And yet not fall; so light is vanity.

ROMEO AND JULIET

Act III · Scene 2

Juliet: Come, night; — come, Romeo; —
*   come, thou day in night;*
For thou wilt lie upon the wings of night
Whiter than new snow on a raven's back. —
Come gentle night, — come, loving, black-brow'd
*   night,*
Give me my Romeo: and, when he shall die,
Take him and cut him out in little stars,
And he will make the face of heaven so fine
That all the world will be in love with night,
And pay no worship to the garish sun.

Nurse: There's no trust,
No faith, no honesty in men; all perjur'd,
All forsworn, all naught, all dissemblers.

Juliet: "Romeo is banished", — to speak that word
Is father, mother, Tybalt, Romeo, Juliet,
All slain, all dead: "Romeo is banished", —
There is no end, no limit, measure, bound,
In that word's death; no words can that woe sound.

Act III · Scene 3

Friar Lawrence: The kind prince,
Taking thy part, hath brush'd aside the law,
And turn'd that black word death to banishment:
This is dear mercy, and thou see'st it not.

194

ROMEO AND JULIET

Act III · Scene 3

Romeo: 'Tis torture, and not mercy: Heaven is here
Where Juliet lives; and every cat and dog,
And little mouse, every unworthy thing,
Live here in heaven, and may look on her;
But Romeo may not.

Act III · Scene 5

Juliet: Wilt thou be gone? it is not yet near day:
It was the nightingale, and not the lark,
That pierc'd the fearful hollow of thine ear;
Nightly she sings on your pomegranate tree:
Believe me, love, it was the nightingale.
Romeo: It was the lark, the herald of the morn,
No nightingale: look, love, what envious streaks
Do lace the severing clouds in yonder east;
Night's candles are burnt out, and jocund day
Stands tiptoe on the misty mountain tops.
I must be gone and live, or stay and die.

Prince Escalus: Go hence, to have more talk of
    these sad things;
Some shall be pardon'd and some punish'd:
For never was a story of more woe
Than this of Juliet and her Romeo.

Timon of Athens · Act V. Scene 1.

Timon: "Come not to me again . . ."

TIMON OF ATHENS

Shakespeare was not a moralist; but evidently the moral climate of the age had a profound effect on his imagination. No less pronounced than the Elizabethans' love of glory was their thirst for power and gold; the great voyages of discovery they carried out had either a commercial or a piratical motive; the Court, though a school of wit and manners, was also the battleground of ambition, envy, greed. The last days of the old Queen had been overclouded; the beginning of the new reign was scarcely more propitious; and it was during this period — between 1601 and 1608 — that Shakespeare wrote his greatest tragedies. Beside *Othello, Lear* or *Macbeth, Timon of Athens* is a minor work — not so much a drama as a succession of diatribes, in which the embittered Athenian rails at length against the general turpitude of mankind. The result is impressive, if slightly monotonous. Coleridge considered that the play was a "lingering vibration of *Hamlet*", and Timon himself "a *Lear* of domestic or ordinary life; — a local eddy of passion on the high road of society . . ." Hazlitt's view was more critical. *Timon,* he wrote, was "the only play of our author in which spleen is the predominant feeling of the mind"; its hero was "tormented with the perpetual contact between things and appearances, between the fresh, tempting outside and the rottenness within . . ." The dramatist's attitude towards the human condition is splenetic rather than deeply tragic; but there is enough of Shakespeare in Timon to make him, now and then, an impassioned lord of language.

TIMON OF ATHENS

Act I · Scene 1

Poet: Our poesy is as a gum, which oozes
From whence 'tis nourished: the fire i'the flint
Shows not till it be struck; our gentle flame
Provokes itself, and, like the current, flies
Each bound it chafes.

Timon: Noble Ventidius! Well;
I am not of that feather to shake off
My friend when he most needs me. I do know him
A gentleman that well deserves a help,

Timon: 'Tis not enough to help the feeble up,
But to support him after.

Old Athenian: One only daughter have I, no kin else,
On whom I may confer what I have got:
The maid is fair, o' the youngest for a bride,
And I have bred her at my dearest cost
In qualities of the best. This man of thine
Attempts her love: I pr'ythee, noble lord
Join with me to forbid him her resort;
Myself have spoken in vain.

TIMON OF ATHENS

Act I · Scene 2

Timon: Nay, my lords, ceremony was but
  devis'd at first
To set a gloss on faint deeds, hollow welcomes,
Recanting goodness, sorry ere 'tis shown;
But where there is true friendship there needs none.
Pray, sit; more welcome are ye to my fortunes
Than my fortunes to me.

Flavius: He is so kind that he now
Pays interest for't; his land's put to their books.
Well, would I were gently put out of office
Before I were forc'd out!
Happier is he that has no friend to feed
Than such that do e'en enemies exceed.
I bleed inwardly for my lord.

Act III · Scene 5

Alcibiades: For pity is the virtue of the law,
And none but tyrants use it cruelly.

Act V · Scene 1

Timon: Come not to me again: but say to Athens,
Timon hath made his everlasting mansion
Upon the beached verge of the salt flood;
Who once a day with his embossed froth
The turbulent surge shall cover: thither come,
And let my grave-stone be your oracle.

Julius Caesar · Act IV. Scene 3.

Brutus: "How ill this taper burns!"

JULIUS CAESAR

In September, 1599, a German tourist recorded that he had just seen, at a London playhouse, a play about "the first Emperor, Julius Caesar", which included some fifteen characters and was wound up with "a lively jig". This may well have been Shakespeare's tragedy, from which a contemporary writer quotes in 1601; and it seems clear that the dramatist's treatment of his subject was influenced by the decline and fall of Essex, who fell into disgrace towards the end of 1599 and, in February, 1601, met his death upon the scaffold. The drama is one "of dark conspiracy and of noble idealism". Brutus, the greatest Roman, is a doomed but splendid personage; while Caesar himself is compared now to a Colossus, now to a royal stag pulled down by princely hunters. Of the last scene between Brutus and Cassius, Coleridge observed that he knew "no part of Shakespeare that more impresses on me the belief of his genius being superhuman . . ." Shakespeare's homosexual tendencies may perhaps be over-emphasised; but male friendships were evidently a subject that he had always found absorbing; and Brutus' affection for Cassius provided him with the material for a particularly poignant episode. None of Shakespeare's other dramas deals quite so exclusively with the world of men. It lacks a villain; each of the protagonists, as the action rolls on, exhibits some heroic qualities; and Antony, when he speaks of the fallen Brutus, describes him as a complete Renaissance hero, whose attributes were blended to form an almost perfect whole:

"His life was gentle, and the elements
So mix'd in him that Nature might stand up
And say to all the world 'This was a man!'"

JULIUS CAESAR

Act I · Scene 2

Soothsayer: Beware the ides of March.
Caesar: What man is that?
Brutus: A soothsayer bids you beware the ides of
*   March.*

Cassius: The fault, dear Brutus, is not in our stars,
But in ourselves, that we are underlings.
Brutus and Caesar: what should be in that Caesar?
Why should that name be sounded more than yours?
Write them together, yours is as fair a name;
Sound them, it doth become the mouth as well.

Julius Caesar: Let me have men about me that are fat;
Sleek-headed men, and such as sleep o'nights:
Yond Cassius has a lean and hungry look;
He thinks too much: such men are dangerous.

Julius Caesar: Yet if my name were liable to fear,
I do not know the man I should avoid
So soon as that spare Cassius. He reads much;
He is a great observer, and he looks
Quite through the deeds of men; he loves no plays,
As thou dost, Anthony; he hears no music;
Seldom he smiles;

Cassius: Therefore it is meet
That noble minds keep ever with their likes;
For who so firm that cannot be seduc'd?

JULIUS CAESAR

Act I · Scene 3

Cassius: And why should Caesar be a tyrant then?
Poor man! I know he would not be a wolf,
But that he sees the Romans are but sheep:
He were no lion, were not Romans hinds.
Those that with haste will make a mighty fire
Begin it with weak straws: what trash is Rome.

Act II · Scene 1

Brutus: The abuse of greatness is, when it disjoins
Remorse from power:

Lucius: This paper, thus seal'd up, and I am sure
It did not lie there when I went to bed.
Brutus: Get you to bed again: it is not day.
Is not to-morrow, boy, the ides of March?

Portia: What, is Brutus sick, —
And will he steal out of his wholesome bed,
To dare the vile contagion of the night,
And tempt the rheumy and unpurg'd air
To add unto his sickness?

Portia: Within the bond of marriage, tell me, Brutus,
Is it excepted I should know no secrets
That appertain to you? Am I yourself
But as it were in sort or limitation, —
To keep with you at meals, comfort your bed,
And talk to you sometimes?

JULIUS CAESAR

Act II · Scene 2

Caesar: Cowards die many times before their deaths;
The valiant never taste of death but once.

Act III · Scene 2

Antony: Moreover, he hath left you all his walks,
His private arbours, and new-planted orchards
On this side Tiber: he hath left them you,
And to your heirs forever, — common pleasures,
To walk abroad, and recreate yourselves.
Here was a Caesar! when comes such another?

Act IV · Scene 2

Brutus: When love begins to sicken and decay,
It useth an enforced ceremony.
There are no tricks in plain and simple faith:

Act IV · Scene 3

Brutus: Remember March, the ides of March
*   remember!*
— — —

Brutus: There is a tide in the affairs of men
Which, taken at the flood, leads on to fortune;
Omitted, all the voyage of their life
Is bound in shallows and in miseries.

JULIUS CAESAR

Act IV · Scene 3

Cassius: Come, Antony, and young Octavius, come,
Revenge yourselves alone on Cassius,
For Cassius is a-weary of the world;
Hated by one he loves; brav'd by his brother;
Check'd like a bondman; all his faults observed,
Set in a note-book, learn'd, and conn'd by rote,
To cast into my teeth. O, I could weep
My spirit from mine eyes!

Act V · Scene 1

Brutus: Why, then, lead on. —
*   O that a man might know*
The end of this day's business ere it come!
But it sufficeth that the day will end,
And then the end is known. — Come, ho! away!

Act V · Scene 5

Antony: This was the noblest Roman of them all:
All the conspirators, save only he,
Did that they did in envy of great Caesar:
He only, in a general honest thought,
And common good to all, made one of them.
His life was gentle; and the elements
So mix'd in him that Nature might stand up
And say to all the world, This was a man!

MACBETH

We owe the plot of *Macbeth*, probably written between 1605 and 1606, to a freak of royal taste. Queen Elizabeth's successor, James I, was passionately interested in the Black Arts, and had himself composed a learned volume on the subject of modern demonology. Shakespeare therefore presented a drama that dealt with witches and the part they were believed to have played in the early history of the King's own line. He gave his material, however, a highly characteristic turn. We have no reason to suppose that Shakespeare ever doubted the real existence of supernatural beings; but his vision of Evil was no means limited to his ideas of Hell and Heaven. In *Macbeth* evil is omnipresent, both in men and women, with their cunning and cruelty, and in the very air we breathe. "It is certainly indicative", remarks Professor Spurgeon, "that there are only two plays in which the word 'love' occurs so seldom . . . and no play in which 'fear' occurs so often". Apprehension and suspicion pervade the atmosphere:

> *Foul whisp'rings are abroad: unnatural deeds*
> *Do breed unnatural troubles: infected minds*
> *To their deaf pillows will discharge their secrets . . .*

Macbeth sinks beneath the burden of guilt, haunted by "terrible dreams" and the unending "torture of the mind". Yet the tyrant is not an unadmirable character — brave, eloquent, energetic, deeply devoted to his even more determined wife, whose resolution at first exceeds his, but whose spirit breaks before his own. Finally, he determines that he must fight to a finish:

> *They have tied me to a stake; I cannot fly,*
> *But bear-like I must fight the course.*

Here it is worth noting that the Globe Theatre was within earshot of the Bear Garden, in which bears and bulls were regularly baited, amid the clamour of ferocious mastiffs and the noisy plaudits of the London mob.

MACBETH

Act I · Scene 3

Macbeth: Speak if you can; — what are you?
First Witch: All hail, Macbeth! hail to thee, thane of
*   Glamis!*
Second Witch: All hail, Macbeth! hail to thee,
*   Thane of Cawdor!*
Third Witch: All hail, Macbeth! that shall be king
*   hereafter!*

Macbeth: This supernatural soliciting
Cannot be ill, cannot be good: — if ill,
Why hath it given me earnest of success,
Commencing in a truth? I am Thane of Cawdor:
If good, why do I yield to that suggestion
Whose horrid image doth unfit my hair,
And make my seated heart knock at my ribs,
Against the use of nature?

Banquo: New honours come upon him,
Like our strange garments, cleave not to their mould
But with the aid of use.
Macbeth: Come what come may,
Time and the hour runs through the roughest day.

Macbeth · Act I. Scene 3.

Macbeth: "Speak if you can;—what are you?"

MACBETH

Act I · Scene 4

Duncan, King of Scotland: There's no art
To find the mind's construction in the face:

Duncan: *Sons, kinsmen, thanes,*
And you whose places are the nearest, know
We will establish our estate upon
Our eldest, Malcolm; whom we name hereafter
The Prince of Cumberland, which honour must
Not unaccompanied invest him only,
But signs of nobleness, like stars, shall shine
On all deservers.

Act I · Scene 6

Banquo: *This guest of summer,*
The temple-haunting martlet, does approve,
By his lov'd mansionry, that the heaven's breath
Smells wooingly here: no jutty, frieze, buttress,
Nor coigne of vantage, but this bird hath made
His pendant bed and procreant cradle:
Where they most breed and haunt, I have observ'd
The air is delicate.

MACBETH

Act I · Scene 7

Macbeth: *If the assassination*
Could trammel up the consequence, and catch,
With his surcease, success; that but this blow
Might be the be-all and the end-all here,
But here, upon this bank and shoal of time, —
We'd jump the life to come.

Macbeth: Away, and mock the time with fairest show:
False face must hide what the false heart doth know.

Act II · Scene 1

Macbeth: Now o'er the one-half world
Nature seems dead, and wicked dream abuse
The curtain'd sleep; now witchcraft celebrates
Pale Hecate's offerings; and wither'd murder,
Alarum'd by his sentinel, the wolf,
Whose howl's his watch, thus with his stealthy place,
With Tarquin's ravishing strides, towards his design
Moves like a ghost.

Act II · Scene 2

Macbeth: Methought I heard a voice cry,
    "Sleep no more!
Macbeth does murder sleep", — the innocent sleep:
Sleep that knits up the ravell'd sleave of care,
The death of each day's life, sore labour's bath,
Balm of hurt minds, great nature's second course,
Chief nourisher in life's feast.

MACBETH

Act III · Scene 2

Macbeth: There's comfort yet; they are assailable;
Then be thou jocund: ere the bat hath flown
His cloister'd flight; ere, to black Hecate's summons,
The shard-borne beetle, with his drowsy hums,
Hath rung night's yawning peal, there shall be done
A deed of dreadful note.

Macbeth: Light thickens; and the crow
Makes wing to the rooky wood:
Good things of day begin to droop and drowse;
Whiles night's black agents to their prey do rouse.

Act IV · Scene 3

Malcolm: Devilish Macbeth
By many of these trains hath sought to win me
Into his power, and modest wisdom plucks me
From over-credulous haste: but God above
Deal between thee and me! for even now
I put myself to thy direction and
Unspeak mine own detraction.

MACBETH

Act V · Scene 1

Lady Macbeth: Here's the smell of the blood still, all the perfumes of Arabia will not sweeten this little hand. Oh, oh, oh!

Act V · Scene 2

Angus: Now does he feel
His secret murders sticking on his hands;
Now minutely revolts upbraid his faith-breach;
Those he commands move only in command,
Nothing in love.

Act V · Scene 3

Macbeth: I have liv'd long enough: my way of life
is fall'n into the sear, the yellow leaf;
And that which should accompany old age,
As honour, love, obedience, troops of friends,
I must not look to have;

Macbeth: Canst thou not minister to a mind diseas'd;
Pluck from the memory a rooted sorrow;
Raze out the written troubles of the brain;
And with some sweet oblivious antidote
Cleanse the stuff'd bosom of that perilous stuff
Which weighs upon the heart?

MACBETH

Act V · Scene 3

Macbeth: That lies like truth: "Fear not, till
      Birnam wood
Do come to Dunsinane", — and now a wood
Comes towards Dunsinane. — Arm, army and out!
If this whitch he avouches does appear,
There is no flying hence nor tarrying here.
I 'gin to be a-weary of the sun,
And wish th'estate o'th' world were now undone.

Act V · Scene 5

Macbeth: Life's but a walking shadow; a poor player,
That struts and frets his hour upon the stage,
And then is heard no more: it is a tale
Told by an idiot, full of sound and fury,
Signifying nothing.

Act V · Scene 7

Macbeth: They have tied me to a stake;
      I cannot fly,
But, bear-like, I must fight the course.

Act V · Scene 8

Macbeth: Why should I play the Roman fool, and die
On mine own sword? whiles I see lives, the gashes
Do better upon them.

Hamlet, prince of Denmark · Act I. Scene 1.

Horatio: "Stay, illusion! If thou hast any sound or use of voice, speak to me . . ."

214

HAMLET

The origins of *Hamlet* are dark and mysterious; a drama depicting the tragedy of the Prince of Denmark was already popular in 1589. Shakespeare seems to have resurrected this old "revenge play" and given it a modern shape. The result is a stratification, incorporating old and new; Hamlet must originally have feigned madness because only if he were believed to be mad could he elude the palace-guards and assassinate his uncle. From these hints Shakespeare built up his inimitable portrait of a supremely introspective and indecisive character. Again he was indebted to his study of Essex; and the resemblance between Hamlet and Essex has frequently been pointed out. Essex himself was a scholar and dilettante who attempted to become a man of action. He, too, had a variously gifted temperament —

> *The courtier's, soldier's, scholar's, eye, tongue, sword,*
> *Th'expectancy and rose of the fair state . . .*

— and combined intellectual seriousness with a touch of moral levity. The *Hamlet* we know was presented on the London stage soon after Essex's tragic fall; and, since its first appearance, it has been endlessly discussed and appraised by writers as diverse as Voltaire (who denounced it as *"une pièce grossière et barbare"*), Samuel Johnson and the late T. S. Eliot. It is a less complete play, though often more exciting, than *Macbeth, Julius Caesar* or *Coriolanus*. It is also full of contemporary allusions. The Prince, in the rôle of "malcontent", was a recognisable Elizabethan type, the returned traveller, addicted to melancholy, who exhibited his embittered disposition in ungartered hose and folded arms. At the same time, Shakespeare adds some references to the contemporary "Stage War", occasioned by the rise of the boyactors — "an aery of children, little eyases" — who then threatened the livelihood of Shakespeare's company.

HAMLET, PRINCE OF DENMARK

Act I · Scene 1

Bernardo: 'Tis now stuck twelve; get thee to bed, Francisco.
Francisco: For this relief much thanks: 'tis bitter cold,
And I am sick of heart.
Bernardo: Have you had quiet guard?
Francisco: Not a mouse stirring.

Horatio: What art thou, that usurp'st this time of
    night.
Together with that fair and warlike form
In which the majesty of buried Denmark
Did sometimes march? by heaven
I charge thee, speak!

Horatio: Now, sir, young Fortinbras,
Of unimproved mettle hot and full,
Hath in the skirts of Norway, here and there.
Shark'd up a list of landless resolutes,
For food and diet, to some enterprise
That hath a stomach in't:

Horatio: I have heard,
The cock, that is the trumpet to the morn,
Doth with his lofty and shrill-sounding throat
Awake the god of day;

HAMLET, PRINCE OF DENMARK

Act I · Scene 1

Marcellus: It faded on the crowing of the cock.
Some day, that ever 'gainst that season comes
Wherein our Saviour's birth is celebrated,
The bird of dawning singeth all night long:
And then, they say, no spirit dare stir abroad;
The nights are wholesome; there no planets strike,
No fairy takes, nor witch hath power, to charm.

Act I · Scene 2

King: How is it that the clouds still hang on you?
Hamlet: Not so, my lord; I am too much i'th' sun.
Queen: Good Hamlet, cast thy nighted colour off,
And let thine eye look like a friend of Denmark.
Do not for ever with thy vailed lids
Seek for thy noble father in the dust.

Hamlet: O, that this too too solid flesh would melt,
Thaw, and resolve itself into a dew!
Or that the Everlasting had not fix'd
His canon 'gainst self-slaughter!

Hamlet: And yet, within a month, —
Let me not think on't, — Frailty, thy name is woman! —

HAMLET, PRINCE OF DENMARK

Act I · Scene 2

Hamlet: That it should come to this!
But two months dead! — nay, not so much, not two;
So excellent a king; that was, to this,
Hyperion to a satyr: so loving to my mother,
That he might not between the winds of heaven
Visit her face too roughly. Heaven and earth!
Must I remember?

Hamlet: How weary, stale, flat, and unprofitable
Seem to me all the uses of this world!

King: And now Laertes, what's the news with you?
You told us of some suit; what is't, Laertes?
You cannot speak of reason to the Dane,
And lose your voice: what would'st thou beg, Laertes
That shall not be my offer nor thy asking?

Hamlet: Foul deeds will rise,
Though all the earth o'erwhelm them, to men's eyes.

HAMLET, PRINCE OF DENMARK

Act I · Scene 3

Laertes: But you must fear,
His greatness weigh'd, his will is not his own;
For he himself is subject to his birth:
He may not, as unvalu'd persons do,
Carve for himself;

Polonius: Beware
Of entrance to a quarrel; but, being in,
Bear't that the opposed may beware of thee.
Give every man thy ear, but few thy voice:
Take each man's censure, but reserve thy judgment.
Costly thy habit as thy purse can buy,
But not express'd in fancy; rich, not gaudy:
For the apparel oft proclaims the man;
And they in France of the best rank and station
Are most select and generous chief in that.
Neither a borrower nor a lender be;
For loan oft loses both itself and friend:
And borrowing dulls the edge of husbandry.
This above all, — to thine own self be true;
And it must follow, as the night the day,
Thou canst not then be false to any man.

HAMLET, PRINCE OF DENMARK

Act I · Scene 3

Ophelia: He hath, my lord, of late made many tenders
Of his affection to me.
Polonius: Affection! pooh! you speak like a green girl,
Unsifted in such perilous circumstance
Do you believe his tenders, as you call them?
Ophelia: I do not know, my lord, what I should think.

Polonius: Ay, springes to catch woodcocks. I do know,
When the blood burns, how prodigal the soul
Lends the tongue vows:

Act I · Scene 4

Hamlet: This heavy-headed revel east and west
Makes us traduc'd and tax'd of other nations:
They clepe us drunkards, and with swinish phrase
Soil our addition.

HAMLET, PRINCE OF DENMARK

Act I · Scene 4

Horatio: Have after. — To what issue will this come?
Marcellus: Something is rotten in the state of
Denmark.

Act I · Scene 5

Ghost: Sleeping within my orchard,
My custom always in the afternoon,
Upon my secure hour thy uncle stole,
With juice of coursed hebenon in a vial,
And in the porches of mine ears did pour
The leperous distilment; whose effect
Holds such an enmity with blood of man
That, swift as quicksilver, it courses through
The natural gates and alleys of the body.

Hamlet: There are more things in heaven and earth,
*   Horatio,*
Than are dreamt of in your philosophy.

HAMLET, PRINCE OF DENMARK

Act II · Scene 1

Polonius:　　　　*See you now;*
Your bait of falsehood takes this carp of truth:
And thus do we of wisdom and of reach,
With windlaces, and with assays of bias,
By indirections find directions out:

The King: He tells me, my sweet queen —
*　　that he hath found*
The head and source of all your son's distemper.
The Queen: I doubt it is no other but the main,
His father's death and our o'erhasty marriage.

Act II · Scene 2

Polonius: Good madam, stay awhile: I will be faithful.
[reads]:
*　　"Doubt thou the stars and fire;*
*　　Doubt that the sun doth move;*
*　　Doubt truth to be a liar;*
*　　But never doubt I love.*
O dear Ophelia, I am ill at these numbers; I have not
art to reckon my groans; but that I love thee best,
O most best believe it. Adieu.
Thine evermore, most dear lady, whilst this machine
is to him. Hamlet".

HAMLET, PRINCE OF DENMARK

Act II · Scene 2

*Polonius [aside]: Though this be madness, yet there is
method in 't. Will you walk out of the air my lord?
Hamlet: Into my grave?
Polonius: Indeed, that is out o' th' air. — [aside] How
pregnant sometimes his replies are! a happiness that
often madness hits on.*

*Hamlet: I have of late, — but wherefore I know not, —
lost all my mirth, forgone all custom of exercises;
and, indeed, it goes so heavily with my disposition that
this goodly frame, the earth, seems to me a sterile
promontory; this most excellent canopy, the air, look
you, this brave o'erhanging firmament, this majestical
roof fretted with golden fire, — why it appears no
other thing to me than a foul and pestilent
congregation of vapours. What a piece of work is
man! How noble in reason! how infinite in faculties!
in form and moving, how express and admirable! in
action, how like an angel! in apprehension, how like a
god! the beauty of the world! the paragon of animals!
And yet, to me, what is this quintessence of dust?
man delights not me; no, nor woman either, though
by your smiling you seem to say so.*

HAMLET, PRINCE OF DENMARK

Act II · Scene 2

Hamlet: What's the news?
Rosenkranz: None, my lord, but that the world's
grown honest.
Hamlet: Then is doomsday near: but your news is not
true.

Hamlet: Why, what an ass am I! This is most brave,
That I, the son of a dear father murder'd,
Prompted to my revenge by heaven and hell,
Must, like a whore, unpack my heart with words,
And fall a-cursing like a very drab,
A scullion!

Guildenstern: For the very substance of the ambitious
is merely the shadow of a dream.
Hamlet: A dream itself is but a shadow.

Polonius: My lord, I will use them according to their
desert.
Hamlet: Odd's bodikin, man, better: use every man
after his desert, and who should scape whipping? Use
them after your own honour and dignity:

HAMLET, PRINCE OF DENMARK

Act III · Scene 1

The Queen: And for your part, Ophelia, I do wish
That your good beauties be the happy cause
Of Hamlet's wildness: so shall I hope your virtues
Will bring him to his wonted way again,
To both your honours.

Hamlet: To be, or not to be, — that is the question: —
Whether 'tis nobler in the mind to suffer
The slings and arrows of outrageous fortune,
Or to take arms against a sea of troubles,
And by opposing end them? — To die, — to sleep, —
No more; and by a sleep to say we end
The heartache and the thousand natural shocks
That flesh is heir to, — 'tis a consummation
Devoutly to be wish'd. To die, — to sleep; —
To sleep! perchance to dream:

Hamlet: And thus the native hue of resolution
Is sicklied o'er with the pale cast of thought;

Ophelia: Take these again; for to the noble mind
Rich gifts wax poor when givers prove unkind.

Ophelia: I was the more deceived.
Hamlet: Get thee to a nunnery: why wouldst thou be a
breeder of sinners? I am myself indifferent honest: but
yet I could accuse me of such things that it were better
my mother had not borne me.

HAMLET, PRINCE OF DENMARK

Act III · Scene 2

Hamlet: *For thou hast been*
As one, in suffering all, that suffers nothing;
A man that Fortune's buffets and rewards
Hast ta'en with equal thanks: and bless'd are those
Whose blood and judgment are so well commingled
That they are not a pipe for Fortune's finger
To sound what stop she please.

Hamlet: Lady, shall I lie in your lap?
Ophelia: No, my lord.
Hamlet: I mean my head upon your lap?
Ophelia: Ay, my lord.
Hamlet: Do you think I meant country matters?

Hamlet: O heavens! die two months ago, and not
forgotten yet? Then there's hope a great man's
memory may outlive his life half a year.

Player King: But what we do determine, oft we break.
Purpose is but the slave to memory;

HAMLET, PRINCE OF DENMARK

Act III · Scene 3

King: *What if this cursed hand*
Were thicker than itself with brother's blood, —
Is there not rain enough in the sweet heavens
To wash it white as snow? Whereto serves mercy
But to confront the visage of offence?

The King: My words fly up, my thoughts remain
    below:
Words without thoughts never to heaven go.

Act III · Scene 4

The Queen: O, Hamlet thou hast cleft my heart in
    twain.
Hamlet: O, throw away the worser part of it,
And live the purer with the other half.
Good night: but go not to my uncle's bed.

HAMLET, PRINCE OF DENMARK

Act III · Scene 4

Hamlet: So again, good night.
I must be cruel, only to be kind,
Thus bad begins and worse remains behind. —

Act IV · Scene 5

Ophelia [*sings*]*:*
>   *To-morrow is Saint Valentine's day*
>   *All in the morning betime,*
>   *And I a maid at your window,*
>   *To be your Valentine.*
>
>   *Then up he rose, and down'd his clothes*
>   *And dupp'd the chamber-door;*
>   *Let in the maid, that out a maid*
>   *Never departed more.*

HAMLET, PRINCE OF DENMARK

Act IV · Scene 5

The King: O Gertrude, Gertrude,
When sorrows come, they come not single spies,
But in battalions!

Laertes: Nature is fine in love; and where 'tis fine
It sends some precious instance of itself
After the thing it loves.

Ophelia: There's rosemary, that's for remembrance;
pray, love, remember: and there is pansies, that's for
thoughts.

HAMLET, PRINCE OF DENMARK

Act IV · Scene 7

The King: *The queen his mother*
Lives almost by his looks; and for myself, —
My virtue or my plague, be it either which, —
She's so conjunctive to my life and soul,
That, as the star moves not but in his sphere,
I could not but by her.

The King: But that I know love is begun by time;
And that I see, in passages of proof,
Time qualifies the spark and fire of it.

Act V · Scene 1

Hamlet: Imperious Caesar, dead and turn'd to clay,
Might stop a hole to keep the wind away:
O, that that earth which kept the world in awe
Should patch a wall t' expel the winter's flaw! —

The Queen: Sweets to the sweet: farewell!
I hop'd thou shouldst have been my Hamlet's wife,
I thought thy bride-bed to have deck'd, sweet maid,
And not have strew'd thy grave.

HAMLET, PRINCE OF DENMARK

Act V · Scene 1

Hamlet: I lov'd Ophelia; forty thousand brothers
Could not, with all their quantity of love,
Make up my sum. — What wilt thou do for her?

Act V · Scene 2

Hamlet: *Rashly,*
And prais'd be rashness for it, — let us know,
Our indiscretion sometimes serves us well,
When our deep plots do fail: and that should teach us
There's a divinity that shapes our ends,
Rough-hew them how we will.

Hamlet: *O, I die, Horatio;*
The potent poison quite o'er-crows my spirit:
I cannot live to hear the news from England;
But I do prophesy th' election lights
On Fortinbras: he has my dying voice:
So tell him, with the occurrents, more and less,
Which have solicited. — The rest is silence.
Horatio: Now cracks a noble heart. — Good-night,
    sweet prince,
And flights of angels sing thee to thy rest!

King Lear · Act III. Scene 2.

King Lear: "Blow, winds, and crack your cheeks! rage! blow!"

KING LEAR

The story of *King Lear* was taken by the dramatist from the *Chronicles* of Holinshed, who had himself derived this ancient legend from the works of a twelfth-century chronicler. Lear is said to have originated in Lir, a formidable Celtic sea-god; and it has been suggested that his daughters were goddesses of the winds, Regan and Goneril being evil storm-winds, and Cordelia the gentle breeze. Though Shakespeare knew nothing of Celtic myth, he gave his drama a primeval colouring. Its atmosphere is dim and cold and harsh; the landscapes it presents are dark and rugged. Lear has a primitive energy; the passions of his two unkind daughters recall the strength of untamed natural forces. Yet — such was Shakespeare's art — Lear is an individual, a pettish, selfish, ill-tempered patriarch, whose own inveterate egotism excites his daughter's cruelty. The poet, we learn from *The Sonnets*, often dreaded growing old; and here is old age at its worst and gloomiest. As a comment on the human condition in general, *King Lear* is Shakespeare's most despairing play. Man is "a poor, bare, forked animal"; the world is the playground of unbridled appetites; amid the uproar of the storm, when the old king is finally driven mad, human existence becomes witches' sabbath:

> *Behold yond simp'ring dame,*
> *Whose face between her forks presages snow . . .*
> *The fitchew nor the soiled horse goes to't*
> *With riotous appetite.*
> *Down to the waist they are centaurs,*
> *Though women all above.*

King Lear was produced about 1606; and at that time, according to some critics, Shakespeare was close to a physical and nervous breakdown.

KING LEAR

Act I · Scene 1

*Earl of Gloster: But I have a son, sir, by order of law,
some year elder than this, who yet is no dearer in my
account: though this knave came something saucily
into the world before he was sent for, yet was his
mother fair; there was good sport at his making, and
the whoreson must be acknowledged.*

*King Lear: Know that we have divided
In three our kingdom: and 'tis our fast intent
To shake all cares and business from our age;
Conferring them on younger strengths, while we
Unburden'd crawl toward death.*

*King Lear: Nothing will come of nothing;
        speak again.
Cordelia: Unhappy that I am, I cannot heave
My heart into my mouth: I love your majesty
According to my bond; nor more nor less.*

*King Lear: The bow is bent and drawn, make from
        the shaft.*

— — —

*Earl of Kent: What wouldst thou do, old man?
Think'st thou that duty shall have dread to speak
When power to flattery bows? To plainness
        honour's bound
When majesty falls to folly.*

KING LEAR

Act I · Scene 1

Goneril: The best and soundest of his time hath been but rash; then must we look to receive from his age, not alone the imperfections of long-ingrafted condition, but therewithal the unruly waywardness that infirm and choleric years bring with them.

Cordelia: Time shall unfold what plighted cunning hides:
Who cover faults, at last shame them derides.
Well may you prosper!

Act I · Scene 2

Edmund: My father compounded with my mother under the dragon's tail; and my nativity was under ursa major; so that it follows, I am rough and lecherous, — Tut, I should have been that I am, had the maidenliest star in the firmament twinkled on my bastardizing — Edgar! Pat, he comes like the catastrophe of the old comedy.

Edmund: A credulous father! and a brother noble,
Whose nature is so far from doing harms
That he suspects none; on whose foolish honesty
My practices ride easy! — I see the business.

KING LEAR

Act I · Scene 3

Goneril: *Idle old man,*
That still would manage those authorities
That he hath given away! — Now, by my life,
Old fools are babes again; and must be us'd
With checks as flatteries, — when they are seen
    abus'd.

Act I · Scene 4

King Lear: Who wouldst thou serve?
Kent: You.
King Lear: Dost thou know me, fellow?
Kent: No, sir; but you have that in your counternance
which I would fain call master.
King Lear: What's that?
Kent: Authority.

King Lear: How old art thou?
Kent: Not so young, sir, to love a woman for singing;
nor so old to dote on her for anything: I have years on
my back forty-eight.

King Lear: Dost thou call me fool, boy?
Fool: All thy other titles thou hast given away; that
thou wast born with.

KING LEAR

Act I · Scene 5

Fool: Canst tell how an oyster makes his shell?
King Lear: No.
Fool: Nor I neither; but I can tell why a snail has a
house.
King Lear: Why?
Fool: Why, to put's head in; not to give it away to his
daughters, and leave his horns without a case.

Act II · Scene 4

Regan: O, sir, you are old;
Nature in you stands on the very verge
Of her confine: you should be rul'd, and led
By some discretion, that discerns your state
Better than you yourself.

KING LEAR

Act II · Scene 4

King Lear: You heavens, give me that patience,
*   patience I need!*
You see me here, you gods, a poor old man,
As full of grief as age; wretched in both!
If it be you that stir these daughters' hearts
Against their father, fool me not so much
To bear it tamely; touch me with noble anger.

Act III · Scene 4

King Lear: Why, thou wert better in thy grave than to
answer with thy uncovered body this extremity of the
skies. — Is man no more than this? Consider him well.
Thou owest the worm no silk, the beast no hide, the
sheep no wool, the cat no perfume. — Ha! here's three
on's are sophisticated! — Thou art the thing itself:
unaccommodated man is no more but such a poor,
bare, forked animal as thou art. — Off, off, you
lendings! — Come, unbutton here.

KING LEAR

Act IV · Scene 1

Edgar: *To be worst,*
The lowest and most dejected thing of fortune,
Stands still in esperance, lives not in fear:
The lamentable change is from the best;
The worst returns to laughter.

Gloster: As flies to wanton boys are we to the gods, —
They kill us for their sport.

Act IV · Scene 6

King Lear: If thou wilt weep my fortunes, take my
        eyes.
I know thee well enough; thy name is Gloster:
Thou must be patient; we came crying hither:
Thou know'st, the first time that we smell the air
We wawl and cry.

Act V · Scene 2

Edgar: What, in ill thoughts again? Men must endure
Their going hence, even as their coming hither:
Ripeness is all.

Othello, The Moor of Venice · Act V. Scene 2.

Othello: "It is the cause, it is the cause, my soul . . ."

OTHELLO

First performed in the Banqueting House, Whitehall, on November 1st, 1604, *Othello* bears little resemblance to its immediate predecessor, *Hamlet*. The story is simple, the action straightforward: Shakespeare develops a single theme — that of romantic love, which turns to murderous jealousy — without complication or digression.

Othello himself is a particularly single-minded character; and it is to his simplicity that he owes his downfall. Whereas Hamlet is a man of divided impulses, both in fortune and in misfortune, Othello has a "one-track mind". When he loves, as when he serves the state, he does so with whole-hearted vigour; and, had his nature been less direct and resolute, he might have remained the Republic's honoured general.

Iago, on the other hand, the "honest fellow" who engineers his ruin, is an essentially dubious and ambiguous personage. Critics have often asked if he fully understands his own actions. Coleridge, for example, believed that he lacked a motive, apart from a deep-rooted love of evil, and that his ingenious attempts to explain his conduct somehow never ring true; while Hazlitt regarded him as a crazy aesthete, entirely indifferent to moral considerations, "an amateur of tragedy in real life . . ." *Othello* is a psychological drama, with a marvellous framework of poetic eloquence. Few of Shakespeare's characters are more eloquent; whether he is describing his youth, bidding his wife farewell or speaking of the sword he wears, he instantly becomes a poet. In some respects, this is the most completely beautiful, as well as the most poignant, of all Shakespearean plays; and it is not surprising that it should have formed the basis of one of the most beautiful of nineteenth-century operas.

OTHELLO, THE MOOR OF VENICE

Act I · Scene 1

Iago: I follow him to serve my turn upon him:
We cannot all be masters, nor all masters
Cannot be truly follow'd. You shall mark
Many a duteous and knee-crooking knave
That, doting on his own obsequious bondage,
Wears out his time, much like his master's ass,
For naught but provender; and when he's old,
*   cashier'd:*
Whip me such honest knaves. Others there are
Who, trimm'd in forms and visages of duty,
Keep yet their hearts attending on themselves;
And, throwing but shows of service on their lords,
Do well thrive by them, and when they have lin'd their
*   coats,*
Do themselves homage: these fellows have some soul;
And such a one I do profess myself,
For, sir,
It is as sure as you are Roderigo,
Were I the Moor I would not be Iago:
In following him I follow but myself;
Heaven is my judge, not I for love and duty,
But seeming so for my peculiar end:
For when my outward action doth demonstrate
The native act and figure of my heart
In compliment extern, 'tis not long after
But I will wear my heart upon my sleeve
For daws to peck at: I am not what I am.

OTHELLO: THE MOOR OF VENICE

Act I · Scene 3

Brabantio: *A maiden never bold;*
Of spirit so still and quiet, that her motion
Blush'd at herself; and she — in spite of nature,
Of years, of country, credit, everything —
To fall in love with what she fear'd to look on!
It is a judgment maim'd and most imperfect
That will confess perfection so could err
Against all rules of nature.

Othello: I ran it through, even from my boyish days
To the very moment that he bade me tell it:
Wherein I spake of most disastrous chances,
Of moving accidents by flood and field:
Of hairbreadth scapes i' the imminent deadly breach:
Of being taking by the insolent foe,
And sold to slavery; of my redemption thence,
And portance in my travel's history:
Wherein of antres vast and deserts idle,
Rough quarries, rocks, and hills whose heads touch
        heaven,
It was my hint to speak, — such was the process;
And of the Cannibals that each other eat,
The Anthropophagi, and men whose heads
Do grow beneath their shoulders.

OTHELLO, THE MOOR OF VENICE

Act I · Scene 3

*Duke of Venice: When remedies are past, the griefs
    are ended
By seeing the worst, which late on hopes depended.
To mourn at mischief that is past and gone
Is the next way to draw new mischief on.*

*Iago: O villanous! I have looked upon the world for
four times seven years; and since I could distinguish
betwixt a benefit and an injury, I never found man that
knew how to love himself. Ere I would say I would
drown myself for the love of a Guinea-hen, I would
change my humanity with a baboon.*

*Iago: Virtue! a fig! 'tis in oursleves that we are thus
or thus. Our bodies are gardens, to the which our
wills are gardeners; so that if we will plant nettles or
sow lettuce, set hyssop and weed up thyme, supply it
with one gender of herbs or distract it with many,
either to have it sterile with idleness or manured with
industry; why, the power and corrigible authority of
this lies in our wills. If the balance of our lives had not
one scale of reason to poise another of sensuality, the
blood and baseness of our natures would conduct us to
most preposterous conclusions: but we have reason to
cool our raging motions, our carnal stings, our
unbitted lusts; whereof I take this, that you call love,
to be a sect or scion.*

OTHELLO, THE MOOR OF VENICE

Act I · Scene 3

Iago: The Moor is of a free and open nature,
That thinks men honest that but seem to be so;
And will as tenderly be led by the nose
As asses are.

Act II · Scene 1

Othello: O my fair warrior!
Desdemona: My dear Othello!
Othello: It gives me wonder great as my content
To see you here before me. O my soul's joy!
If after every tempest come such calms,
May the winds blow till they have waken'd death!
And let the labouring bark climb hills of seas
Olympus-high, and duck again as low
As hell's from heaven! If it were now to die,
'Twere now to be most happy; for, I fear,
My soul hath her content so absolute
That not another comfort like this
Succeeds in unknown fate.

OTHELLO, THE MOOR OF VENICE

Act II · Scene 3

Cassio: She's a most exquisite lady.
Iago: And, I'll warrant her, full of game.
Cassio: Indeed, she's a most fresh and delicate
creature.
Iago: What an eye she has! Methinks it sounds a
parley to provocation.

Othello: Why, how now, ho! from whence ariseth this?
Are we turn'd Turks, and to ourselves do that
Which Heaven hath forbid the Ottomites?
For Christian shame, put by this barbarous brawl:
He that stirs next to carve for his own rage
Holds his soul light; he dies upon his motion. —
Silence that dreadful bell! it frights the isle
From her propriety. — What is the matter, masters? —
Honest Iago, that look'st dead with grieving,
Speak, who began this? on thy love, I charge thee.

Iago: What, are you hurt, lieutenant?
Cassio: Ay, past all surgery.
Iago: Marry, heaven forbid!
Cassio: Reputation, reputation, reputation! O, I have
lost my reputation! I have lost the immortal part of
myself, and what remains is bestial.

OTHELLO THE MOOR OF VENICE

Act III · Scene 3

Desdemona: When shall he come?
Tell me, Othello: I wonder in my soul
What you would ask me, that I should deny,
Or stand so mammering on.

Othello: I heard thee say even now, thou likedst
*   not that,*
When Cassio left my wife: what didst not like?
And when I told thee he was of my counsel
In my whole course of wooing, thou criedst: "Indeed!"
And didst contract and pursue thy brow together,
As if thou then hadst shut up in thy brain
Some horrible conceit: if thou dost love me,
Show me thy thought.
Iago: Good my lord, pardon me:
Though I am bound to every act of duty,
I am not bound to that all slaves are free to.
Utter my thoughts? Why, say they are vile and false, —
As where's that palace whereunto foul things
Sometimes intrude not? who has a breast so pure
But some uncleanly apprehensions
Keep leets and law-days, and in session sit
With meditations lawful?

Iago: O, beware, my lord, of jealousy;
It is the green-ey'd monster which doth mock
The meat it feeds on:

OTHELLO, THE MOOR OF VENICE

Act III · Scene 3

Othello: *'Tis not to make me jealous*
To say my wife is fair, feeds well, loves company,
Is free of speech, sings, plays and dances well;
Where virtue is, these are more virtuous:
Nor from mine own weak merits will I draw
The smallest fear or doubt of her revolt;
For she had eyes, and chose me. No Iago:
I'll see before I doubt.

Othello: *No, not much mov'd: —*
I do not think but Desdemona's honest.
Iago: Long live she so! and live you to think so!
Othello: And yet, how nature erring from itself,
Iago: Ay, there's the point.

Act III · Scene 3

Othello: *O curse of marriage,*
That we can call these delicate creatures ours,
And not their appetites! I had rather be a toad,
And live upon the vapour of a dungeon,
Than keep a corner in the thing I love
For other's use. Yet 'tis the plague of great ones;
Prerogativ'd are they less than the base.

OTHELLO, THE MOOR OF VENICE

Act III · Scene 3

Othello: *O, now, for ever,*
Farewell the tranquil mind! farewell content!
Farewell the plumed troop and the big wars
That make ambition virtue! O, farewell!
Farewell the neighing steed and the shrill trump,
The spirit-stirring drum, th' ear-piercing fife,
The royal banner, and all quality,
Pride, pomp and circumstance of glorious war!

Act III · Scene 4

Emilia: But jealous souls will not be answer'd so;
They are not ever jealous for the cause,
But jealous for they are jealous: 'tis a monster
Begot upon itself, born on itself.

Act V · Scene 2

Othello [kissing Desdemona]: O balmy breath,
that dost almost persuade,
Justice to break her sword! One more, one more: —
Be thus when thou art dead, and I will kill thee,
And love thee after — one more, and this the last.
So sweet was ne'er so fatal, I must weep,
But they are cruel tears; this sorrow's heavenly,
It strikes where it doth love.

Antony and Cleopatra · Act II. Scene 2.

Enobarbus: "So many mermaids, tended her i' the eyes . . ."

ANTONY AND CLEOPATRA

Here again, as in *Othello*, Shakespeare applied himself to the subject of obsessive sexual passion. Like Othello, the ill-fated Roman is a great and generous character; but he lacks Othello's deep integrity and his beguiling youthful innocence. Whereas Othello has been taken unawares by love, Antony understands his own feelings; but, although he understands them, he cannot control them and drifts half-willingly towards his doom. "Of all Shakespeare's historical plays", wrote Coleridge, *Antony and Cleopatra* was "by far the most wonderful"; and much of its quality was due to "the manner in which the fiery force is sustained throughout, and to the numerous momentary flashes of nature counteracting the historic abstraction". The passion that unites its hero and heroine is neither idealized nor sentimentalized. Cleopatra is a "triumphant lady", who ensnares her lover in a "strong toil of grace". She is also a creature of flesh and blood, not regularly beautiful, no longer very young – she describes herself as "wrinkled deep in time" – but a mature woman of strong and earthy appetites. Shakespeare contrasts the terrestial origins of love with its poetic effect upon the imagination; and the play reaches an imaginative climax when his lovers bid the world farewell. Their love has been a glorious illusion – yet an illusion for which they were glad to exchange reality . . . First produced between 1606 and 1607, towards the close of Shakespeare's penultimate period, *Antony and Cleopatra* inspired John Dryden to write his splendid *Love for Love* – a very different version of the same story, presented on the London stage in 1678.

ANTONY AND CLEOPATRA

Act I · Scene 1

Cleopatra: If it be love, indeed, tell me how much.
Antony: There's beggary in the love that can be
reckon'd.

Antony: Let Rome in Tiber melt, and the wide arch
Of the ranged empire fall! Here is my space.
Kingdoms are clay: our dungy earth alike
Feeds beast as man: the nobleness of life
Is to do thus; when such a mutual pair
And such a twain can do 't.

Act I · Scene 3

Cleopatra: Eternity was in our lips and eyes,
Bliss in our brow's bent; none our parts so poor
But was a race of heaven.

ANTONY AND CLEOPATRA

Act I · Scene 3

Cleopatra: *What should I do, I do not?*
Charmian: In each thing give him way; cross him
    in nothing.
Cleopatra: Thou teachest like a fool, — the way
    to lose him.
Charmian: Tempt him not so too far; I wish, forbear:
In time we hate that which we often fear.

Act I · Scene 4

Caesar: It is not Caesar's natural vice to hate
Our great competitor. From Alexandria
This is the news: — he fishes, drinks, and wastes
The lamps of night in revel; is not more manlike
Than Cleopatra, nor the queen of Ptolemy
More womanly than he.

Act I · Scene 5

Cleopatra: *O Charmian,*
Where think'st thou he is now? Stands he or sits he?
Or does he walk? or is he on his horse?
O happy horse to bear the weight of Antony;
Do bravely horse! for wott'st thou whom thou mov'st?

ANTONY AND CLEOPATRA

Act II · Scene 2

Enobarbus: Never, he will not:
Age cannot wither her, nor custom stale
Her infinite variety: other women cloy
The appetites they feed; but she makes hungry
Where most she satisfies.

Act II · Scene 5

Cleopatra: *Come hither, sir.*
Though it be honest, it is never good
To bring bad news: give to a gracious message
An host of tongues; but let ill tidings tell
Themselves when they be felt.

Act II · Scene 6

Enobarbus: Octavia is of a holy, cold, and still
conversation.
Menas: Who would not have his wife so?
Enobarbus: Not he that himself is not so; which is.
Mark Antony.

ANTONY AND CLEOPATRA

Act II · Scene 7

Caesar: Possess it, I'll make answer:
But I had rather fast from all four days
Than drink so much in one.

Act III · Scene 1

Ventidius: O Silius, Silius,
I have done enough: a lower place, note well,
May make too great an act; for learn this, Silius, —
Better to leave undone, than by our deed
Acquire too high a fame when him we serve's away.

Act III · Scene 6

Caesar: No, my most wronged sister; Cleopatra
Hath nodded him to her. He hath given his empire
Up to a whore; who now are levying
The kings o' the earth for war.

ANTONY AND CLEOPATRA

Act III · Scene 11

Cleopatra: *O my lord, my lord*
Forgive my fearful sails! I little thought
You would have follow'd.
Antony: *Egypt, thou knew'st too well*
My heart was to thy rudder tied by the strings,
And thou shouldst tow me after; o'er my spirit
Thy full supremacy thou knew'st,

Act III · Scene 12

Caesar: To try thy eloquence, now 'tis time: despatch;
From Antony win Cleopatra: promise,
And in our name, what she requires; add more,
From thine inventions, offers: women are not
In their best fortunes strong; but want will perjure
The ne'er touched vestal:

ANTONY AND CLEOPATRA

Act III · Scene 13

Enobarbus: *What though you fled*
From that great face of war, whose several ranges
Frighted each other? why should he follow?

Cleopatra: *Most kind messenger,*
Say to great Caesar this — in deputation
I kiss his conquering hand: tell him, I am prompt
To lay my crown at's feet, and there to kneel:
Tell him, from his all-obeying breath I hear
The doom of Egypt.

Antony: Where hast thou been, my heart?
— Dost thou hear lady?
If from the field I shall return once more
To kiss these lips, I will appear in blood;
I and my sword will earn our chronicle:
There's hope in't yet.

ANTONY AND CLEOPATRA

Act IV · Scene 7

Scarus: *Swallows have built*
In Cleopatra's sails their nests: the augurers
Say they know not, — they cannot tell; — look grimly,
And dare not speak their knowledge. Antony
Is valiant, and dejected; and, by starts,
His fretted fortunes give him hope and fear
Of what he has and has not.

Act IV · Scene 14

Antony: Sometime we see a cloud that's dragonish;
A vapour sometime like a bear or lion,
A tower'd citadel, a pendant rock,
A forked mountain, or blue promontory
With trees upon't, that nod unto the world,
And mock our eyes with air: thou hast seen these signs;
They are black vesper's pageants.

ANTONY AND CLEOPATRA

Act V · Scene 2

Cleopatra: Give me my robe, put on my crown; I have
Immortal longings in me: now no more
The juice of Egypt's grape shall moist this lip: —
Yare, yare, good Iras; quick. — Methinks I hear
Antony call; I see him rouse himself
To praise my noble act; I hear him mock
The luck of Caesar, which the gods give men
To excuse their after wrath. Husband, I come:
Now to that name my courage prove my title!
I am fire and air; my other elements
I give to baser life. — So, — have you done?
Come then, and take the last warmth of my lips.
Farewell, kind Charmian; — Iras, long farewell.

Cleopatra [*To an asp, which she applies to her breast*]:
Come, thou mortal wretch,
With thy sharp teeth this knot intrinsicate
Of life at once untie: poor venomous fool,
Be angry, and despatch. O couldst thou speak,
That I might hear thee call great Caesar ass
Unpolicied!

Cymbeline · Act III. Scene 3.

Belarius with the princes outside the cave.

CYMBELINE

A critic of Shakespeare's last plays has assured us that, in *Cymbeline*, Shakespeare was trying out a new technique, and deserting his early realism for a more symbolic method. But it is equally possible that he had begun to tire of the stage, and that what his admirer acclaims as symbolic subtleties were really signs of lassitude and inattention. The play seems to have been carelessly put together. *Cymbeline*, like *A Winter's Tale*, has the structure of a fairy story, including an ill-used princess and a brace of young princes brought up in a mountain cave by a faithful old servant. Imogen shares some of the charm of Perdita; but Perdita would not have mistaken the headless body of Cloten, a man she despised and detested, for that of her beloved husband Posthumus, merely because he had purloined his clothes. When Shakespeare was engaged on *Cymbeline*, he already contemplated retirement from the stage; and soon afterwards, during the year 1611, he sold the valuable shares he held in the Globe and the Blackfriars Theatre, preparatory to withdrawing into private life. But, if he was abandoning his craft, he had not forgotten his art. He continued to weave his old poetic spell; and *Cymbeline* has rare poetic moments. The poetry, however, appears to have been imposed on the play rather than to arise naturally from the evolution of the drama.

CYMBELINE

Act I · Scene 1

First gentleman: He that hath miss'd the princess
        is a thing
Too bad for bad report:

First gentleman: I do not think
So fair an outward and such stuff within
Endows a man but he.

Imogen: Dissembling courtesy! How fine this tyrant
Can tickle where she wounds! — My dearest husband,
I something fear my father's wrath; but nothing —
Always reserv'd my holy duty — what
His rage can do on me. You must be gone:
And I shall here abide the hourly shot
Of angry eyes.

Act I · Scene 5

Cornelius [aside]: I do not like her. She doth think
        she has
Strange lingering poisons: I do know her spirit,
And will not trust one of her malice with
A drug of such damn'd nature.

CYMBELINE

Act I · Scene 6

Iachimo: There is a Frenchman his companion, one
An eminent monsieur, that, it seems, much loves
A Gallian girl at home; he furnaces
The thick sighs from him; whiles the jolly Briton —
Your lord I mean — laughs from's free lungs, cries O!

Act II · Scene 2

Iachimo: The crickets sing, and man's o'erlabour'd
    sense
Repairs itself by rest.

Act II · Scene 5

Posthumus: Is there no way for men to be, but women
Must be half-workers? We are all bastards;
And that most venerable man which I
Did call my father was I know not where
When I was stamp'd; some coiner with his tools
Made me a counterfeit: yet my mother seem'd
The Dian of that time: so doth my wife
The nonpareil of this.

CYMBELINE

Act II · Scene 5

Posthumus: Could I find out
The woman's part in me! For there's no motion
That tends to vice in man but I affirm
It is the woman's part: be it lying, note it,
The woman's; flattering, hers; deceiving, hers;
Lust and rank thoughts, hers, hers; revenges, hers;
Ambitions, covetings, change of prides, disdain,
Nice longing, slanders, mutability,
All faults that have a name, nay, that hell knows,
Why, hers, in parts or all; but rather all;

Act III · Scene 2

Imogen: O, for a horse with wings!
Hear'st thou, Pisanio?
He is at Milford-Haven: read and tell me
How far 'tis thither. If one of mean affairs
May plod it in a week, why may not I
Glide thither in a day?

Act III · Scene 6

Imogen: Yes; no wonder
When rich ones scarce tell true: no lapse in fullness
Is sorer than to lie for need, and falsehood
Is worse in kings than beggars, — My dear lord!
Thou art one o' the false ones: now I think on thee
My hunger's gone: but even before, I was
At point to sink for food.

CYMBELINE

Act III · Scene 6

Belarius: Fair youth, come in!
Discourse is heavy, fasting; when we have supp'd
We'll mannerly demand thee of thy story,
So far as thou wilt speak it.

Act IV · Scene 2

Guiderius: Golden lads and girls all must,
As chimney-sweepers, come to dust.

Arviragus: Brother, stay here:
Are we not brothers?
Imogen: So man and man should be;
But clay and clay differs in dignity,
Whose dust is both alike.

Act IV · Scene 3

Pisanio: Wherein I am false I am honest;
*   not true to be true:*

All other doubts, by time let them be clear'd:
Fortune brings in some boats that are not steer'd.

Act V · Scene 1

Posthumus: You some permit
To second ills with ills, each elder worse,
And make them dread it, to the doers' thrift.

TROILUS AND CRESSIDA

Although this tragi-comedy, when first published as a Quarto in 1609, was advertised as an entirely new work, "never staled with the stage", it is thought that *Troilus and Cressida* may well have been written soon after the production of *Julius Caesar*. Again the dramatist's approach to his subject seems to have been influenced by the fall of Essex. In *Julius Caesar*, statesmen and soldiers have still a tragic or heroic dignity; in Shakespeare's drama of the Trojan War, they are either crafty or devious like Ulysses, or brutal and boorish like Achilles, who, having retired from the struggle, lolls on a "lazy bed", exchanging "scurril jests" with his homosexual crony. If the idea of heroism is demolished, so is the conception of love that Shakespeare had developed in such early romantic plays as *Romeo and Juliet*. Love here is prisoner of human failings: "This is the monstruosity in love, lady — that the will is infinite and the execution confined; that the desire is boundless and the act a slave to limit". Troilus and Cressida are the most unadmirable, though not the least interesting, pair of lovers that Shakespeare ever put upon the stage — Cressida, the sexual opportunist who exploits her own attraction; Troilus, a clear-sighted dupe, who admits that his mistress is a "daughter of the game", but continues to demand of her a purity and fidelity that he knows she cannot give. Troilus' fierce jealousy is far more horrifying than that of Othello because he has none of Othello's basic innocence. His passion is a raging, unsatisfied hunger; and it is noteworthy how many of the images that Shakespeare employs in *Troilus and Cressida* are connected with the sense of taste.

266

TROILUS AND CRESSIDA

Prologue: Like, or find fault; do as your pleasures are;
Now good or bad, 'tis but the chance of war.

Act I · Scene 1

Troilus: The Greeks are strong and skilful to their
            strength,
Fierce to their skill, and to their fierceness valiant;
But I am weaker than a woman's tear,
Tamer than sleep, fonder than ignorance,
Less valiant than the virgin in the night,
And skilless as unpractis'd infancy.

Troilus: Tell me, Apollo, for thy Daphne's love,
What Cressid is, what Pandar, and what we
Her bed is India; there she lies, a pearl:
Between our Ilium and where she resides
Let it be call'd the wild and wandering flood;
Ourself the merchant; and this sailing Pandar
Our doubtful hope, our convoy, and our bark.

Act I · Scene 2

Pandarus: You are such a woman! one knows not at
what ward you lie.
Cressida: Upon my back, to defend my belly; upon
my wit, to defend my wiles; upon my secrecy, to
defend mine honesty; my mask, to defend my beauty;
and you, to defend all these: and at all these wards I
lie, at a thousand watches.

Troilus and Cressida · Act 1. Scene 3.

Ulysses: "*The great Achilles,—whom opinion crowns the
sinew and the forehand of our host,—having his ear
full of his airy fame, grows dainty of his worth, and
in his tent lies mocking our designs . . .*"

TROILUS AND CRESSIDA

Act I · Scene 2

Cressida: Things won are done, joy's soul lies
*   in the doing:*
That she belov'd knows naught that knows not this, —
Men prize the thing ungain'd more than it is:
That she was never yet that ever knew
Love got so sweet as when desire did sue:

Act I · Scene 3

Ulysses: And 'tis this fever that keeps Troy on foot,
Not her own sinews. To end a tale of length
Troy in our weakness stands, not in her strength.
Nestor: Most wisely hath Ulysses here discover'd
The fever whereof all our power is sick.
Agamemnon: The nature of the sickness found,
*   Ulysses,*
What is the remedy?

Ulysses: They tax our policy, and call it cowardice;
Count wisdom as no member of the war;
Forestall prescience, and esteem no act
But that of hand.

TROILUS AND CRESSIDA

Act II · Scene 2

Priam: Thus once again says Nestor from the Greeks:—
"Deliver Helen, and all damage else, —
As honour, loss of time, travail, expense,
Wounds, friends, and what else dear that is consum'd
In hot digestion of this cormorant war, —
Shall be struck off".

Hector: 'Tis mad idolatry
To make the service greater than the god;

Troilus: Nay if we talk of reason
Let's shut our gates and sleep!

Cassandra: Cry, Trojans, cry! practise your eyes with
*   tears!*
Troy must not be, nor goodly Ilion stand;

Act II · Scene 3

Ullyses: The elephant hath joints, but none for courtesy:
his legs are legs for necessity, not for flexure.

Agamemnon: He that is proud eats up himself; pride
is his own glass, his own trumpet, his own chronicle;
and whatever praises itself but in the deed devours the
deed in the praise.

TROILUS AND CRESSIDA

Act III · Scene 1

*Pandarus: Is this the generation of love? hot blood,
hot thoughts, and hot deeds? Why, they are vipers:
is love a generation of vipers? —*

Act III · Scene 2

*Cressida: But though I lov'd you well, I woo'd you not;
And yet, good faith, I wish'd myself a man,
Or that we women had men's privilege
Of speaking first.*

*Troilus: No, Pandarus: I stalk about her door,
Like a strange soul upon the Stygean banks
Staying for waftage.*

Act IV · Scene 4

*Troilus: Cressid, I love thee in so strain'd a purity
That the blest gods, — as angry with my fancy,
More bright in zeal than the devotion which
Cold lips blow to their deities, — take thee from me.*

*Troilus: Injurious time now, with a robber's haste,
Crams his rich thievery up, he knows not how:
As many farewells as be stars in heaven,
With distinct breath and consign'd kisses to them,
He fumbles up into a loose adieu;
And scants us with a single famish'd kiss,
Distasted with the salt of broken tears,*

THE SONNETS

Shakespeare's *Sonnets* have been likened to a haunted cavern, with innumerable footprints scattered around its entrance, showing that many explorers have crossed its threshold, but that none of them has yet emerged. The problem they present seems almost insoluble. When the sequence was first published, apparently without the author's leave, in May or June, 1609,

272

the printer included a highly mysterious dedication — to a certain "Mr. W.H.", whom he describes as "the onlie begetter of these insuing sonnets", and wishes "all happinesse and that eternitie promised by our ever-living poet". Mr. W.H. has not yet been satisfactorily identified; and it has been suggested by some critics that he was not the "begetter" of the poems in the sense that he inspired them, but may merely have given them life by procuring and handing over Shakespeare's manuscript. Though the poems contain traditional elements, borrowed from ancient and modern literature, they also tell an extremely personal story. The poet loves a handsome, well-bred youth, whom he courts, flatters and admonishes; at the same time, he has a dark, attractive mistress; and his mistress betrays him with his friend. He and the golden youth he loves occupy very different social stations; and the poet is obliged to practice a somewhat ignominious calling, which takes him up and down the country. Who was Shakespeare's beloved if not Southampton, a brilliant, extravagant, capricious young man, the patron addressed both in *Venus and Adonis* and in *The Rape of Lucrece?* Southampton's character exactly fits him for the part; and we know that he was once accused of displaying homosexual tendencies. *The Sonnets* are a monument to homosexual love; though the poet insists that his passion is platonic, and that he expects no physical return. Just as the story of the *Sonnets* has provoked endless discussion, so has the problem of their dating. Probably begun as early as 1594 or 1595, they seem to include references to the death of Queen Elizabeth in 1603. Some years before they had been published, we learn, Shakespeare's "sugared sonnets" were already well-known among his "private friends". During the seventeenth century they were much admired — in 1640 an editor calls them *"serene,* clear and elegantly plain"; but eighteenth-century critics considered them perversely obscure; and not until the opening of the nineteenth century, when they were praised by Keats and Wordsworth, did they arouse speculation as well as admiration. With the help of the sonnet, Wordsworth declared, Shakespeare had "unlocked his heart". Today we feel that he did not unlock it completely, but afforded us a fascinating glimpse of a strange personal drama that he could not quite disclose.

SONNETS

Sonnet 17

Who will believe my verse in time to come,
If it were filled with your most high deserts?
Though yet, Heaven knows, it is but as a tomb
Which hides your life, and shows not half your parts.
If I could write the beauty of your eyes,
And in fresh numbers number all your graces,
The age to come would say, "This poet lies,
Such heavenly touches ne'er touch'd earthly faces?

Sonnet 34

Why didst thou promise such a beauteous day,
And make me travel forth without my cloak,
To let base clouds o'ertake me in my way,
Hiding thy bravery in their rotten smoke?
'Tis not enough that through the cloud thou break,
To dry the rain on my storm-beaten face,
For no man well of such a salve can speak,
That heals the wound and cures not the disgrace.

Sonnet 40

Take all my loves, my love, yea take them all:
What hast thou then more than thou hadst before?
No love, my love, that thou mayst true love call;
All mine was thine before thou hadst this more.
Then if for my love thou my love receivest,
I cannot blame thee for my love thou usest.

SONNETS

Sonnet 55

Not marble, nor the gilded monuments
Of princes, shall outlive this powerful rhyme;
But you shall shine more bright in these contents
Than unswept stone, besmear'd with sluttish time.

Sonnet 60

Like as the waves make towards the pebbled shore,
So do our minutes hasten to their end;

Sonnet 63

Against my love shall be, as I am now,
With Time's injurious hand crush'd and o'erworn;
When hours have drain'd his blood, and fill'd his brow
With lines and wrinkles;

— — —

Against confounding age's cruel knife,
That he shall never cut from memory
My sweet love's beauty, though my lover's life.

Sonnet 65

Since brass, not stone, nor earth, nor boundless sea,
But sad mortality o'ersways their power,
How with this rage shall beauty hold a plea,
Whose action is no stronger than a flower?

SONNETS

Sonnet 73

That time of year thou mayst in me behold
When yellow leaves, or none, or few, do hang
Upon those boughs which shake against the cold,
Bare ruin'd choirs, where late the sweet birds sang.

Sonnet 104

To me, fair friend, you never can be old,
For as you were when first your eye I eyed,
Such seems your beauty still. Three winters' cold
Have from the forests shook three summers' pride;
Three beauteous springs to yellow autumn turn'd
In process of the seasons have I seen;
Three April perfumes in three hot Junes burn'd,
Since first I saw you fresh, which yet are green.

Sonnet 109

O, never say that I was false of heart,
Though absence seem'd my flame to qualify!
As easy might I from myself depart,
As from my soul, which in thy breast doth lie:
That is my home of love.

SONNETS

Sonnet 130

My mistress' eyes are nothing like the sun;
Coral is far more red than her lips' red;
If snow be white, why then her breasts are dun;
If hairs be wires, black wires grow on her head,
I have seen roses damask'd, red and white,
But no such roses see I in her cheeks

And yet, by heaven, I think my love as rare
As any she belied with false compare.

Sonnet 138

When my love swears that is made of truth,
I do believe her, though I know she lies;
That she might think me some untutor'd youth,
Unlearned in the world's false subtleties.
Thus vainly thinking that she thinks me young,
Although she knows my days are past the best,
Simply I credit her false-speaking tongue;
On both sides thus is simple truth supprest.

Sonnet 150

O, from what power has thou this powerful might,
With insufficiency my heart to sway?
To make me give the lie to my true sight,
And swear that brightness doth not grace the day?

In the letter on the inside of the cover, Shakespeare dedicates his poem to Henry Wriothesly, Earl of Southampton (see page 13). This poem was the first to be printed (in 1593).

CONTENTS

	Page
Introduction by Peter Quennell	3
The Tempest	27
Two Gentlemen of Verona	40
Merry Wives of Windsor	47
Measure for Measure	51
Much Ado About Nothing	60
Love's Labour's Lost	71
A Midsummer Night's Dream	76
The Merchant of Venice	87
As You Like It	102
The Taming of the Shrew	109
All's Well That Ends Well	113
Twelfth Night	119
The Winter's Tale	127
King John	141
Richard II	145
Henry IV	153
Henry V	161
Henry VI	164
Richard III	171
Henry VIII	175
Coriolanus	179
Titus Andronicus	183
Romeo and Juliet	187
Timon of Athens	197
Julius Caesar	201
Macbeth	206
Hamlet	215
King Lear	233
Othello	241
Antony and Cleopatra	251
Cymbeline	261
Troilus and Cressida	266
Sonnets	272